11+ Maths
Word Problems

For GL Assessment

Maths Word Problems are a seriously tricky part of the GL 11+, so we've made a whole book of 10-Minute Tests to help children master them!

Each test is packed with GL-style practice at the perfect level for ages 10-11, all with detailed answers included at the back of the book.
Nobody does 11+ prep better than CGP.

10-Minute Tests

Ages 10-11

How to access your free Online Edition

This book includes a free Online Edition to read on your PC, Mac or tablet. You'll just need to go to **cgpbooks.co.uk/extras** and enter this code:

0150 3638 8852 8068

By the way, this code only works for one person. If somebody else has used this book before you, they might have already claimed the Online Edition.

How to use this book

This book is made up of 10-minute tests and puzzle pages.
There are answers and detailed explanations at the back of the book.

10-Minute Tests

- There are 31 tests in this book, each containing 10 questions.

- Each test is designed to target the type of context-based maths questions that your child could come across in their 11+ test, and covers a variety of topics at the right difficulty levels.

- Your child should aim to score at least 8 out of 10 in each 10-minute test.
  If they score less than this, use their results to work out the areas they need more practice on.

- If your child hasn't managed to finish the test in time, they need to work on increasing their speed, whereas if they have made a lot of mistakes, they need to work more carefully.

- Keep track of your child's scores using the progress chart on the inside back cover of the book.

Puzzle Pages

- There are 12 puzzle pages in this book, which are a great break from test-style questions.
  They encourage children to practise similar skills that they will need in the test, but in a fun way.

Published by CGP

Editors:
Catherine Lear, Hannah Roscoe, Ethan Starmer-Jones, James Summersgill, Sean Walsh

With thanks to Shaun Harrogate and David Ryan for the proofreading.
With thanks to Emily Smith for the copyright research.

ISBN: 978 1 78908 205 0
Printed by Elanders Ltd, Newcastle upon Tyne
Clipart from Corel®

Based on the classic CGP style created by Richard Parsons.

Text, design, layout and original illustrations © Coordination Group Publications Ltd. (CGP) 2018
All rights reserved.

Photocopying this book is not permitted, even if you have a CLA licence.
Extra copies are available from CGP with next day delivery. • 0800 1712 712 • www.cgpbooks.co.uk

Contents

Test 1 2
Test 2 5
Test 3 8
Puzzles 1 11
Test 4 12
Test 5 15
Puzzles 2 18
Test 6 19
Test 7 22
Test 8 25
Puzzles 3 28
Test 9 29
Test 10 32
Puzzles 4 35
Test 11 36
Test 12 39
Test 13 42
Puzzles 5 45
Test 14 46
Test 15 49
Puzzles 6 52

Test 16 53
Test 17 56
Test 18 59
Puzzles 7 62
Test 19 63
Test 20 66
Puzzles 8 69
Test 21 70
Test 22 73
Test 23 76
Puzzles 9 79
Test 24 80
Test 25 83
Puzzles 10 86
Test 26 87
Test 27 90
Test 28 93
Puzzles 11 96
Test 29 97
Test 30 100
Test 31 103
Puzzles 12 106
Answers 107

Test 1

You have **10 minutes** to do this test. Work as quickly and accurately as you can.

1. The mass of a wardrobe is 46.49 kg to the nearest 10 g.
   What is the mass of the wardrobe to the nearest kilogram?

   Answer: _____ kg

2. Vivian has five number cards, shown below.

   She arranges them to make the biggest 5-digit number she can.
   What is this number?

   Answer: _____

3. Steffi is selling raffle tickets. She sells 2.5 books of tickets, each containing 1000 tickets. She sells each ticket for 10p. How much money does she make? Circle the correct option.

   A £25   C £2500   E £2.50
   B £25 000   D £250

Test 1

4. Matt goes to a park and asks dog walkers what the ages of their dogs are in years. The ages are listed here.

> 1, 3, 4, 5, 8, 8, 13

What is the mean age of the dogs? Circle the correct option.

A   8   C   7   E   13
B   6   D   5

5. A librarian noted down the number of pages in 100 books, but she forgot to write down the number of books that had 200-299 pages. She recorded her results in a table, shown below.

Number of pages	Number of books
1-99	4
100-199	15
200-299	?
300-399	19
400-499	22
500-599	30

How many books had fewer than 300 pages?

Answer: _____

6. Jeremy is doing his chores. He spends three quarters of an hour vacuuming, 50 minutes cleaning the bathroom and 25 minutes mowing the lawn. How long does he spend in total doing his chores? Circle the correct option.

A   2 hours
B   1 hour and 45 minutes
C   1 hour and 30 minutes
D   2 hours and 20 minutes
E   2 hours and 45 minutes

7. Rob has a bottle containing 1.5 litres of water. He uses it to water plants. On the first day he uses 100 ml. On the second day he uses 200 ml. He carries on in this pattern, each day using 100 ml more than the day before. After how many days will the bottle be empty?

Answer: _____ days

8. During one week, Sarah went for a run on three days. On the first day she ran 2.3 km, on the second day she ran 3.7 km and on the third day she ran 2 miles. If 1 mile = 1.6 km, how many kilometres did Sarah run in total during that week?

Answer: _____ km

9. Mrs Kahn wants to draw a pie chart to show what the members of her class had for tea last night. 20% of the class had fish and chips. What angle should Mrs Kahn use to show this on the pie chart? Circle the correct option.

   A 50°   C 90°   E 72°
   B 20°   D 105°

10. Arno is an architect. He designs a house with an unusually shaped roof. A cross section of the house is shown below. It shows an isosceles triangle on top of a rectangle

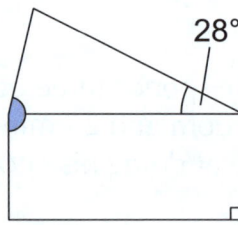

What is the size of the shaded angle?

Answer: _____ °

/ 10

Test 2

You have **10 minutes** to do this test. Work as quickly and accurately as you can.

1. In a lucky dip game, you win a prize if you randomly pick three factors of 24. Which set of three numbers below would win a prize? Circle the correct option.

   A 3, 10, 12   **C** 3, 4, 12   **E** 2, 5, 8
   B 6, 8, 11   **D** 2, 14, 20

2. Teddy is stacking boxes in the sequence shown.

   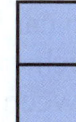 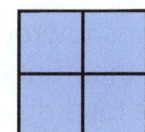 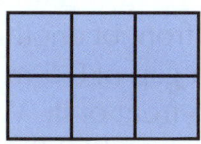

   How many boxes will there be in the stack that is 50 boxes wide?

   Answer: _____

3. Charlie needs to buy some fresh hay to put in the rabbit hutches in a pet shop. 1 bag of hay covers 3 rabbit hutches. How many full bags will he need to buy for 20 hutches?

   Answer: _____

4. Joan is varnishing the floor of her dining room. The floor is a rectangle measuring 5 m × 6 m. One tin of varnish covers an area of 10 m² and costs £4. How much will it cost to varnish the surface of the floor?

   Answer: £ _____

5. Melissa is thinking of a shape, and Joshua is trying to guess it by asking questions. He asks, "Does it have four sides?". Melissa says, "Yes." Which of the following questions does Joshua not now need to ask? Circle the correct option.

   A   Does it have parallel sides?
   B   Is it symmetrical?
   C   Do the angles add up to 360°?
   D   Do any sides have the same length?
   E   Does it have a right angle?

6. Five cars are lined up, one in front of another, in a car showroom. Each car has a length of 4 m, and there is a gap of 0.5 m between the front end of each car and the back end of the car in front of it. What is the total distance between the first and last car, including the length of those cars? Circle the correct option.

   A   19 m   B   21.5 m   C   22.5 m   D   22 m   E   23 m

7. The table shows the number of cups of tea that Scott drinks each day over a week.

Mon	Tues	Wed	Thurs	Fri	Sat	Sun
9	7	5	4	5	2	3

   What is the mean number of cups of tea that Scott drinks from Monday to Friday. Circle the correct option.

   A   4   B   5   C   6   D   7   E   8

8. Hassan recorded the temperature in his garden at different times of the day. In the morning, the temperature was 8 °C. By the afternoon, the temperature had increased by 75%. What was the temperature in the afternoon?

Answer: _____ °C

9. Jerry sells tables that come in boxes measuring 2 m × 1 m × 1 m. He is sending a shipment abroad and hires the shipping container shown in the diagram below.

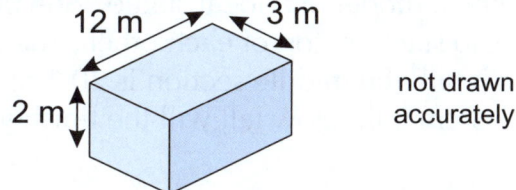

not drawn accurately

How many boxes can Jerry fit in the container?
Circle the correct option.

A   2448
B   144
C   120
D   96
E   36

10. The cost of staying at a campsite is £14 per night for the pitch, plus £4 for each camper. Dogs are permitted, at a cost of £2 per dog per night. Which expression shows the cost per night of staying at the campsite for *c* people and *d* dogs? Circle the correct option.

A $14c + 2d$
B $cd(14 + 4 + 2)$
C $14 + 4c + 2d$
D $14 + (4 + c) + (2 + d)$
E $56c + 28d$

/ 10

Test 3

You have **10 minutes** to do this test. Work as quickly and accurately as you can.

1. Kylie and Thea start counting forward from 10.
   Kylie counts in steps of 4 and Thea counts in steps of 7.
   What is the first number that will appear in both their sequences?

   Answer: _____

2. Parinder is building a model of a local statue. She builds three different sections to stack on top of each other. The bottom section is 17.3 cm tall, the middle section is 20.1 cm tall and the top section is 15.3 cm tall. How tall will the finished model be?

   Answer: _____ cm

3. A group of 39 children were asked whether their birthday this year is on a weekday or at the weekend. Some of the results are shown in the table.

	Boys	Girls	Total
Weekday		16	
Weekend	10		
Total		23	

   How many boys have their birthday on a weekday?

   Answer: _____

4. Derek is making tea in a cafeteria. He uses 2 tea bags for every 3 cups of tea, and makes a total of 72 cups. How many tea bags does he use?

   Answer: _____

5. The pictogram shows how many tickets were sold at a cinema on one day for different types of films.

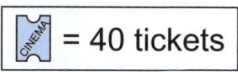 = 40 tickets

Type	Tickets sold
Comedy	🎟🎟🎟🎟🎟
Action	🎟🎟🎟🎟🎟
Drama	🎟
Sci-Fi	🎟🎟🎟

How many tickets were sold for action films?
Circle the correct option.

    A 50   **B** 170   **C** 130   **D** 90   **E** 350

6. A travel card costs £15 and saves $1/3$ of the cost of any journey. A return bus fare from Alice's house to Hulverston costs £1.50. Alice makes this journey every day. How many days will it take for Alice's total savings to equal the price of the travel card? Circle the correct option.

    A 3   **B** 30   **C** 5   **D** 10   **E** 15

7. One year, the 24th October is a Tuesday. What day is the 16th November in the same year? Circle the correct option.

    A Monday   **C** Wednesday   **E** Friday
    B Tuesday   **D** Thursday

8. Clara is buying carrots for ten horses. The carrots come in bags of six. She gives an equal number of carrots to each horse and there are no carrots left over. What is the fewest number of bags of carrots that Clara could have bought?

Answer: _____

9. The diagram below shows two playing blocks stacked together.

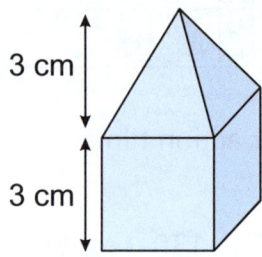

The volume of a square-based pyramid is $\frac{1}{3}$ × area of the base × height. What is the total volume of the two playing blocks? Circle the correct option.

A   36 cm³   C   45 cm³   E   63 cm³
B   27 cm³   D   330 cm³

10. Mr Cox collects action figures. Exactly half of them are still in their original packaging. The other half are not. Out of the ones still in their original packaging, exactly half are limited edition. Which of the following could be the total number of action figures Mr Cox has in his collection? Circle the correct option.

A   55   B   50   C   88   D   63   E   90

Puzzles 1

Now for a break from 10-minute tests. Try out your skills on this puzzle.

Which Planet Next?

Ali the space scout is trying to earn his space orienteering badge. However, he can't figure out which planet he is supposed to be visiting next. The map below shows how far away each planet is. Ali knows that the distance in alien miles between him and the planet he is trying to get to has a:

- 5 in either the tens or ones place.
- 2 in the hundreds place.
- 7 in the ten thousands place.
- 8 in the hundred thousands place.

Circle the planet that Ali needs to visit next.

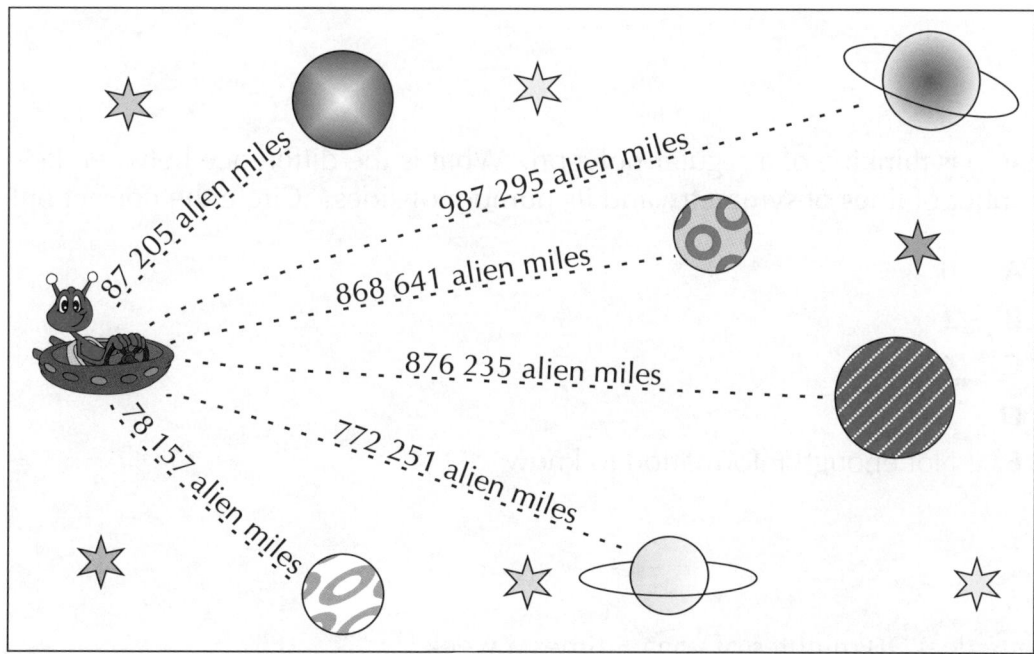

Ali travels a distance of 52 761 alien miles towards the planet you have circled. How far does he have left to travel before reaching the planet?

_____ alien miles

Test 4

You have **10 minutes** to do this test. Work as quickly and accurately as you can.

1. It takes Amber 41 minutes to get home from work.
   She gets home at 6:08 pm. What time does Amber leave work?

   Answer: _____

2. Eliza is selling bottles of strawberry and banana smoothie. She needs to make sure that the amount of smoothie in each bottle is 1000 ml when rounded the nearest 100 ml. Eliza's friend Arizona tells her that one of the bottles will not round to this amount. Which of these is Arizona referring to? Circle the correct option.

   A   1003 ml   C   968 ml   E   1055 ml
   B   1045 ml   D   955 ml

3. Mateo is thinking of a regular polygon. What is the difference between its number of lines of symmetry and its number of sides? Circle the correct option.

   A   0
   B   2
   C   4
   D   5
   E   Not enough information to know

4. Betty does 30 minutes of yoga 5 times a week.
   How many minutes of yoga does she do in 8 weeks?

   Answer: _____ minutes

5. A school votes on what colour they would like their new school tie to be. The results are put in the bar chart.

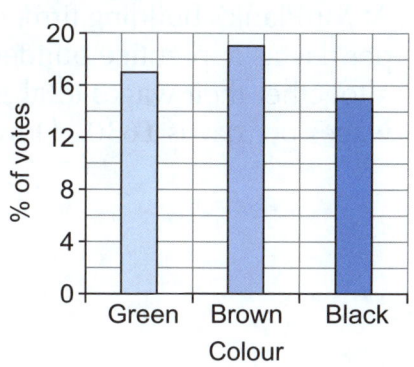

Why is the bar chart misleading? Circle the correct option.

  A No one would choose brown.
  B The colours aren't in order.
  C Not all the votes are shown on the graph.
  D The numbers go up in 4s.
  E The percentages should be on the horizontal axis.

6. A party planner has designed a dance floor made up of white and blue circles. Both circles have the same centre, as shown in the diagram below.

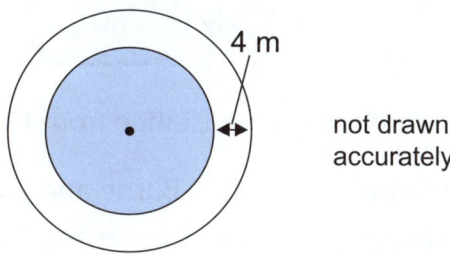

not drawn accurately

If the whole dance floor has a diameter of 30 m, what is the radius of the blue part of the dance floor?

Answer: _____ m

7. At a parents' evening, a teacher sees 20 sets of parents, each for the same amount of time, without any breaks. If the parents' evening is 2 hours 40 minutes long, how long does the teacher see each set of parents for?

Answer: _____ minutes

8. At Mr Plank's building firm, qualified builders get paid three times as much per day as apprentice builders. Mr Plank has 7 apprentice builders and altogether their wages total £210 per day. The total of the qualified builders' wages per day is £630. How many qualified builders work at the firm?

Answer: _____

9. Darren is driving and sees the sign below. It shows the distance in km to six towns that are all along the same straight road.

> Arch 22
> Barne 32.5
> Copp 39
> Drise 41.5
> Erton 45.5
> Flynn 50

Which two towns are the same distance from Copp? Circle the correct option.

A Arch and Drise   C Barne and Drise   E Arch and Flynn
B Arch and Erton   D Barne and Erton

10. A bakery is planning to expand their business. They use the formula $5n^2 - 3n$ to work out how many scones they aim to have sold in total by the end of each day, where n stands for the number of days since the bakery started expanding. How many scones do they aim to have sold in total by the end of the 10th day?

Answer: _____

/ 10

Test 5

You have **10 minutes** to do this test. Work as quickly and accurately as you can.

1. A chocolate bar weighs 50 grams. It contains 5 grams of fat.
   What percentage of the chocolate bar is fat? Circle the correct option.

   A 10%   **C** 5%   **E** 45%
   B 1%   **D** 0.1%

2. Laura goes to the gym every four days. Kelvin goes to the gym every five days. If they both go to the gym today, after how many days will they both go to the gym on the same day again?

   Answer: _____ days

3. Alessia draws a line from point *M* that crosses the line *AB* at a 90° angle.

   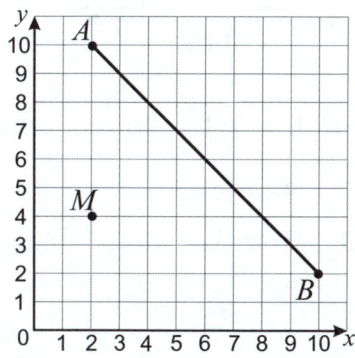

   At what point does the line she draws cross *AB*?
   Circle the correct option.

   A (8, 4)   **C** (5, 7)   **E** (6, 6)
   B (2, 10)   **D** (7, 5)

4. Simon went out for a meal. His main course cost £8.95, his dessert cost £3.69 and his drink cost £1.35.
He paid with a £20 note. How much change did he get?

Answer: £ _____

5. Angela has a block of clay that weighs 15 kg. She makes clay bowls that weigh 500 g, that can each hold 300 ml of water. If no clay is wasted, how many litres of water can Angela's bowls hold in total?

Answer: _____ litres

6. The floor plan of a room is shown in the diagram below.

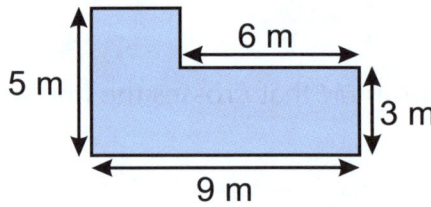

What is the area of the room? Circle the correct option.

- **A** 45 m²
- **B** 27 m²
- **C** 33 m²
- **D** 36 m²
- **E** 23 m²

7. The time, in seconds, taken to prepare and serve a hot lunch in a factory canteen is given by the formula $20W + 1200$. W is the number of workers having a hot lunch. How many seconds would it take to prepare and serve a hot lunch for 20 workers?

Answer: _____ seconds

8. Lukas bought 6 bags of dog food to share equally between 15 dogs. What fraction of 1 bag should each dog get? Circle the correct option.

   A ²/₃   B ⁴/₉   C ³/₄   D ²/₅   E ½

9. A class of 30 children were asked to name an orange vegetable. The results are shown in the pie chart below.

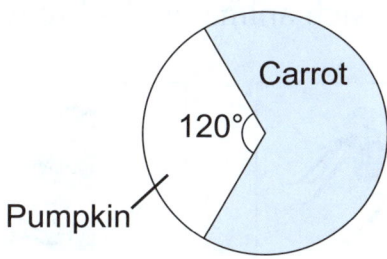

How many children said carrot?

Answer: _____

10. A builder sets up a pulley system to lift steel beams up to the top of a building. The pulley can lift a maximum of 65 kg in one go. Each beam has a mass of 7 kg. How many times will the builder need to raise the pulley to lift 100 beams? Circle the correct option.

    A 3   B 12   C 10   D 15   E 11

Puzzles 2

Now for a break from 10-minute tests. Try out your skills on these puzzles.

Time For a Brew

Hetty is making a potion. The potion needs to contain exactly 44 legs, 6 tails and 4 wings. Using the information below, work out how many of each animal Hetty needs to put in the potion. There must be at least one of each animal in the brew.

2 wings
2 legs
1 tail

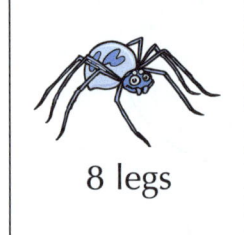
8 legs

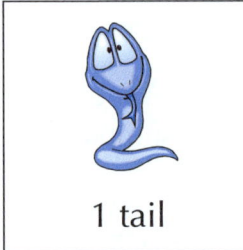
1 tail

4 legs
1 tail

Bat: _____   **Spider:** _____   **Snake:** _____   **Lizard:** _____

Herbal Medication

Hetty wants to make the potion stronger by adding in a 45 g mixture of dangerous ingredients. This mixture should be 6 parts hemlock, 4 parts crow feathers and 5 parts thistle. If the ratio isn't correct, the potion will become poisonous. How many grams of each ingredient does Hetty need, in order to make 45 g of the mixture?

Hemlock: _____ g   **Crow feathers:** _____ g   **Thistle:** _____ g

Test 6

You have **10 minutes** to do this test. Work as quickly and accurately as you can.

1. A group of children are playing 'pin the tail on the donkey'.
   The table shows how far each player pinned the tail from the correct point.

	Distance (m)
Rhys	1.45
Marshall	0.21
Emilia	1.10
Ceri	0.35
Dan	0.19

   Who was closest to the correct point? Circle the correct option.

   A Rhys   **D** Ceri
   B Marshall   **E** Dan
   C Emilia

2. Joy is buying petrol at 112.3 pence per litre. How much, in pounds, will it cost to buy 30 litres of petrol? Circle the correct option.

   A £0.33   **C** £3.31   **E** £3369
   B £33.69   **D** £330.69

3. Jeff was born on a Tuesday. Jim was born 30 days after Jeff. On what day of the week was Jim born?

   Answer: _____

4. A coin is tossed so that it lands heads or tails on either a red mat or a blue mat. Some of the results of tossing the coin 31 times have been recorded in the table.

	Heads	Tails	Total
Red	5		19
Blue			
Total	14		31

How many times did the coin land showing tails on the blue mat?

Answer: _____

5. The diagram below shows a number sequence arranged into ascending steps. The number at the top of the first step is 1, the number at the top of the second step is 3, and the number on the top of the third step is 6.

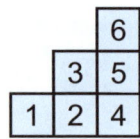

What number will be at the top of the fifth step?

Answer: _____

6. A flower grows 8 mm per month. It was 8 cm tall when Ashok bought it, and it has since grown to a height of 12.8 cm.
How long has Ashok had the flower? Circle the correct option.

A 6 months   D 12 months
B 3 months   E 8 months
C 5 months

7. Jacqueline is wrapping presents. She starts with one sheet of wrapping paper. She uses $\frac{1}{5}$ of the sheet to wrap a box of chocolates and $\frac{3}{10}$ of the sheet to wrap a book. What percentage of the wrapping paper is left over?

Answer: _____ %

8. Toni is building a cuboid for a school project. She creates a frame by bending pieces of wire to create the edges of the cuboid, as shown.

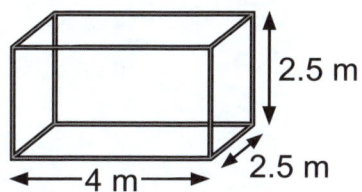

What is the total length of wire she has used to make the frame?

Answer: _____ m

9. The cost of taking luggage on an aeroplane is £15, plus £Y for every kilogram the luggage weighs over 20 kg. Which of these expressions gives the cost in pounds of taking a 24 kg suitcase on board? Circle the correct option.

    A $15 + 4Y$ D $4(15 + Y)$
    B $24 + 15Y$ E $(15 + 24)Y$
    C $4Y - 15$

10. Pedro buys a tie in a sale. He pays £16 for the tie, which has been reduced from its original price of £20. By what percentage has the price of the tie been reduced? Circle the correct option.

    A   15%   D   30%
    B   40%   E   25%
    C   20%

/ 10

Test 7

You have **10 minutes** to do this test. Work as quickly and accurately as you can.

1. Anna rounds the number 4 230 850 to the nearest thousand. What is the value of the 1 in the new rounded number? Circle the correct option.

    A one million   C one thousand   E one hundred
    B ten thousand   D ten

2. Les makes the shape shown on the right out of identical cubes.

    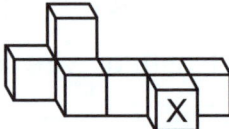

    Which of the following shows the shape as seen directly from the front, so that the X is viewed head-on? Circle the correct option.

    A    C 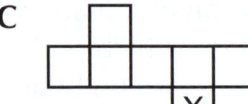   E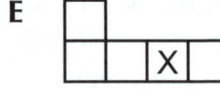

    B 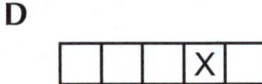   D

3. A recipe for a fruit salad uses the ratio 2:5 for the proportion of apples to oranges. Ruth puts 6 apples in her fruit salad. How many oranges does she use?

    Answer: _____

4. Penny is walking her dog. They walk 2 miles to the beach.
They then take a different route back home, which is 3.4 km long.
If 1 mile = 1.6 km, how far does Penny walk her dog? Give your answer in km.

Answer: _____ km

5. The advertisement shown is from local newspaper 'The Daily Scoop'.

> **More People Read The Daily Scoop**
> 70% of people surveyed said they read The Daily Scoop — only three out of every four people surveyed said they read The Morning Cable.

Why is the advertisement misleading? Circle the correct option.

    A   It doesn't say how many people were surveyed.
    B   It doesn't say if people read any other newspapers than the two mentioned.
    C   According to the survey, more people actually read The Morning Cable.
    D   The survey says each newspaper is read by the same number of people.
    E   The Daily Scoop wrote the advertisement, so they must have made it up.

6. Fluffy drinks 20% more milk than Mrs Tibbles.
Mrs Tibbles drinks 350 ml of milk. How much milk does Fluffy drink?

Answer: _____ ml

7. Alain is setting out seats for a concert. The front row contains the fewest seats, then the other rows each have an equal number of seats. There are 154 seats altogether, spread across 13 rows. The front row contains 10 seats.
How many seats are in each of the other rows? Circle the correct option.

    A 11   **C** 13   **E** 15
    B 12   **D** 14

8. Five identical isosceles triangles are arranged to create a star, as shown below. Each isosceles triangle has a base length of 10 cm and a perimeter of 26 cm.

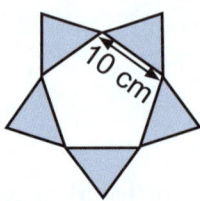

The bases of the triangles form a regular pentagon.
What is the perimeter of the star?

Answer: _____ cm

9. Arran wins £150. He gives 5 of his friends £P each. Which expression shows how much money he has left over, in pounds? Circle the correct option.

   A   150 – P
   B   5P
   C   150 – 5P
   D   150P
   E   100 + 5P

10. Mr Klein's car will travel 39.5 miles for every gallon of fuel used. He rounds this to the nearest mile before estimating the amount of fuel he needs for a 440 mile trip.

   His car has exactly the amount of fuel that he estimated he would need.
   How many miles short of his destination will this amount of fuel get him?
   Circle the correct option.

   A   55 miles
   B   0.55 miles
   C   5.5 miles
   D   0.055 miles
   E   5 miles

/ 10

Test 8

You have **10 minutes** to do this test. Work as quickly and accurately as you can.

1. The number of cakes a bakery sold during one month is 3820 to the nearest 10. What is the largest number of cakes that could have been sold during this time?

   Answer: _____

2. Mrs Finch herds the same number of cows into a field every hour. The table below shows how many cows were in the field each hour.

Time	Cows
08:00	148
09:00	159
10:00	170
11:00	181
12:00	

   How many cows will there be in the field at midday?

   Answer: _____

3. Rosie is stacking boxes. The greatest number of boxes which can be stacked safely in one pile is 7. There are 100 boxes to stack altogether. How many boxes will be left over once they have been stacked into piles of 7?

   Answer: _____

4. Mrs Stone's class made a bar chart to show their favourite colours, but they forgot to put numbers on the scale. The most popular colour was chosen by 12 pupils. How many pupils chose blue?

   Answer: _____

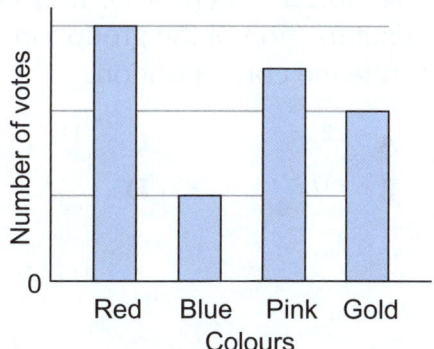

5. John thinks of a number between 30 and 39 and counts backwards in steps of 7. He reaches the number 5. What number did he start from?

Answer: _____

6. Kamal records the number of bike rides 8 people went on in a month. He puts his data in the sorting diagram below.

	?	?
Factor of 12	2 3	4 6
Not a factor of 12	5 7	8 9

Which of the following could be the two missing labels from Kamal's sorting diagram? Circle the correct option.

- **A** Not a square number / Square number
- **B** Odd / Even
- **C** Whole number / Not a whole number
- **D** Prime number / Not a prime number
- **E** Factor of 21 / Not a factor of 21

7. A group of pupils took part in a sponsored run. The table shows how far they each ran. What fraction of the group ran 300 m or less? Circle the correct option.

- **A** $2/3$
- **B** $1/3$
- **C** $11/15$
- **D** $5/6$
- **E** $3/4$

Distance (m)	Number of pupils
1-100	4
101-200	6
201-300	12
301-400	8

Test 8

8. Caitlin buys 2 bottles of water and 3 pieces of the same type of fruit from the menu shown on the right. She spends £2.15. Which fruit did she buy? Circle the correct option.

Healthy Menu	
Bottled Water	55p
Apple	70p
Banana	35p
Peach	45p
Plum	25p
Orange	40p

   A   Apple
   B   Banana
   C   Peach
   D   Plum
   E   Orange

9. A town council is building a mountain biking track at a local youth centre. Part of the design for the track is shown below.

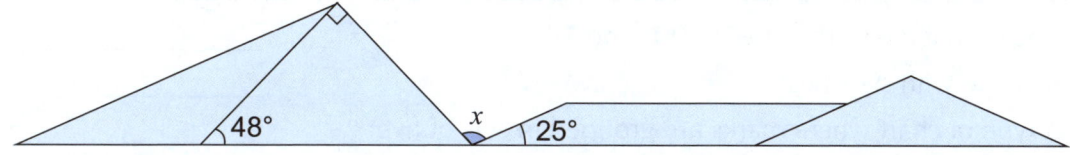

What is the size of the angle marked x?

Answer: _____ °

10. Skye draws a series of identical squares on the axes below. The coordinates of one corner are shown.

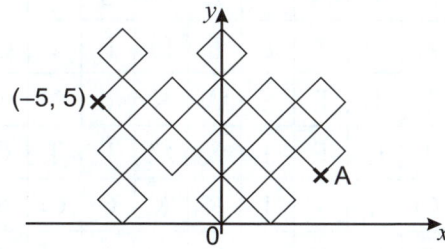

What are the coordinates of point A? Circle the correct option.

   A   (2, 1)
   B   (4, 2)
   C   (2, 4)
   D   (2, 2)
   E   (5, 5)

/ 10

Puzzles 3

Now for a break from 10-minute tests. Try out your skills on this puzzle.

Termsearch

Use the clues in the box below to write down eight mathematical words, then find these words in the wordsearch — some words are written backwards or diagonally. Be careful though, the wordsearch has other mathematical words too.

Clues:

a) Angles that measure between 90° and 180°: _____
b) A shape with six sides: _____
c) A type of chart where marks are grouped in sets of five: _____
d) A type of chart where pictures are used to represent amounts: _____
e) A 2D shape which can be folded to create a 3D shape: _____
f) A type of triangle that has no equal sides or angles: _____
g) A sensible guess at an answer (often used with rounding): _____
h) A type of maths where symbols, such as letters, are used to represent unknown quantities, such as numbers: _____

T	E	A	R	H	K	Q	A	P	N	F	Z	W	S	P	Z	Q	E	B	B	R	T
Q	A	L	G	E	B	R	A	P	Z	E	E	D	E	I	O	P	B	P	A	V	T
S	N	L	I	T	C	E	L	F	E	S	W	R	L	C	S	C	A	L	E	N	E
E	R	R	L	K	D	N	I	U	E	T	X	M	E	T	C	G	O	J	G	J	V
V	T	I	O	Y	P	W	O	I	I	K	K	C	O	N	A	O	J	Q	Q	V	
G	T	U	B	M	C	J	P	G	Q	M	U	C	S	G	A	R	D	E	C	J	A
D	W	E	C	Z	Z	H	W	O	A	A	N	Q	O	R	B	A	H	H	I	S	Z
A	U	O	N	A	X	B	A	Y	Q	T	R	C	S	A	H	T	T	I	M	E	O
S	N	O	I	T	R	O	P	R	R	E	P	R	I	M	G	C	R	S	G	A	J
E	S	U	T	B	O	H	Y	C	T	A	L	E	N	O	G	A	X	E	H	Y	T
S	R	O	T	C	A	F	K	F	V	S	U	O	H	S	M	G	C	N	A	F	S

Test 9

You have **10 minutes** to do this test. Work as quickly and accurately as you can.

1. Lucia enters a javelin competition. She needs to throw the javelin 40 m to qualify for the second round. She throws the javelin 38.4 m. How far short is she from qualifying?

    Answer: _____ m

2. Pablo is looking at his school timetable. He has six 50-minute lessons per day. How many hours does he spend in lessons each day?

    Answer: _____ hours

3. A group of friends are dividing themselves into groups for a sports tournament. They can divide themselves into 8 groups of 7. How many groups of 4 could they divide themselves into?

    Answer: _____

4. Tamim wants to buy a circular paddling pool that is 3.5 m wide. He calls a shop to ask for sizes. The shop gives him the sizes for the five different paddling pools they sell. Which paddling pool is the size Tamim wants? Circle the correct option.

    A   radius = 7 m
    B   diameter = 1.75 m
    C   radius = 1.75 m
    D   diameter = 7 m
    E   radius = 3.5 m

5. A crisp company did a survey of 100 people to find their favourite crisp flavour. 25% chose cheese and onion, 53 chose salt and vinegar and the rest chose ready salted. How many people chose ready salted?

Answer: _____

6. A teacher asked some pupils to write down fractions slightly larger than 1. All but one of the pupils wrote down fractions which had the same value. Which of these fractions is not equivalent to the others? Circle the correct option.

    A $50/45$ C $20/18$ E $40/36$

    B $30/27$ D $11/9$

7. Sam's teacher says: "6450 divided by 30 equals 215". His teacher then asks for the answer to 215 multiplied by 60. Which of the following could Sam use to correctly answer this question? Circle the correct option.

    A   64 500   C   1290   E   12 450

    B   12 900   D   3225

8. Daphné is fitting an island in her kitchen. The diagram shows the floor plan for the fitting. What will the area of the remaining floor space be once the island has been fitted? Circle the correct option.

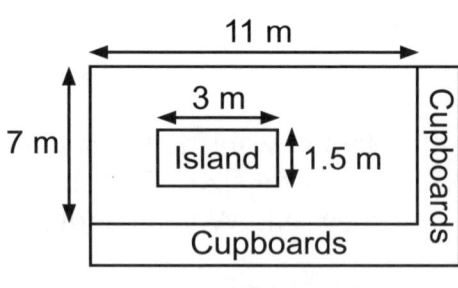

not drawn accurately

    A   77 m²   D   81.5 m²

    B   73.5 m²   E   72.5 m²

    C   4.5 m²

9. Four friends eat 23 pieces of fruit between them in a week.
A chart is drawn to show the number of pieces of fruit eaten by each of them.

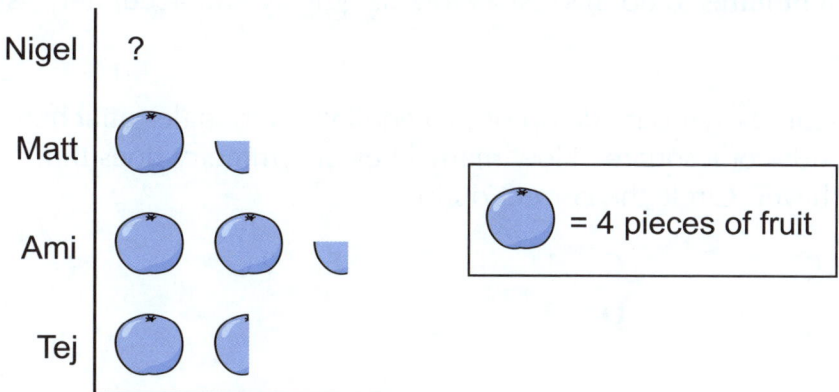

Which of the following should be drawn in Nigel's row to complete the chart? Circle the correct option.

A   B   C   D   E

10. Jenny and Iman each have a bag of sweets. Each bag contains the same number of sweets. Jenny gives $1/3$ of her sweets to Sara and Iman gives $1/6$ of her sweets to Sara. Which of these statements is now true? Circle the correct option.

    A   Jenny has more sweets than Iman.
    B   Sara has more sweets than Jenny.
    C   Sara has half as many sweets as Iman.
    D   Iman has more sweets than Sara.
    E   Jenny has twice as many sweets as Sara.

/ 10

Test 10

You have **10 minutes** to do this test. Work as quickly and accurately as you can.

1. The shape shown is made up of two equilateral triangles attached to the sides of a square. How many lines of symmetry does the shape have? Circle the correct option.

    A   0   C   1   E   2
    B   3   D   4

   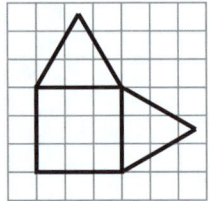

2. Gwen is taking part in a quiz. For every right answer, she gets one point. For every wrong answer, she loses one point. She gets 12 answers correct and 15 answers wrong. What is her final score? Circle the correct option.

    A   12   C   −15   E   27
    B   −12   D   −3

3. Jenna buys a ribbon of length 2.5 m. She divides it equally into shorter ribbons of length 10 cm. How many pieces of ribbon does she now have?

    Answer: _____

4. A bottle of milk costs £1.45. An office orders 4 bottles of milk on Monday, 4 bottles of milk on Wednesday, and 2 bottles of milk on Friday. How much did they spend on milk that week?

    Answer: £ _____

5. Kym has a bag of marbles. They can't be divided into equal groups. Which of the following could be the number of marbles Kym has? Circle the correct option.

   A 14   B 21   C 39   D 41   E 49

6. Kieran's age is exactly divisible by 6 and 9.
   Two years ago, his age was a square number.
   How old is Kieran? Give your answer in years.

   Answer: _____ years

7. At the end of the year, Lauren counted the number of bike rides she went on during each season. She records the results in a pictogram.

Season	Number of bike rides
Spring	4½ wheels
Summer	5½ wheels
Autumn	4 wheels
Winter	1¼ wheels

   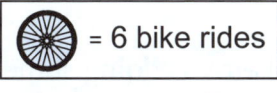 = 6 bike rides

   How many more bike rides did she go on during summer than winter? Circle the correct option.

   A 28   C 21   E 14
   B 26   D 19

8. Bernard recorded the length of time it took five people to swim 500 m.

Amelia	7 minutes
Samuel	10 minutes
Carolina	12 minutes
Arizona	8 minutes
Violet	

The mean length of time it took them to swim 500 m was 9 minutes. How long did it take Violet to swim 500 m?

Answer: _____ minutes

9. A bus sets off from Millon at 5 minutes past and 35 minutes past every hour. It stops at Grizebell 20 minutes after leaving Millon. It takes Lena 10 minutes to walk from home to the bus stop at Millon. She is meeting a friend outside Grizebell bus station at 11:00. What is the latest time she could leave home to arrive in time to meet her friend? Circle the correct option.

A 09:55   **C** 10:25   **E** 09:25
B 10:05   **D** 10:35

10. Leroy is doing some sale shopping. He finds two jackets that are on sale.

Smart Togs
Original Price: £55
Now: 20% OFF!

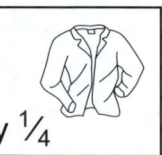
Top Garms
Was: £60
Now: Reduced by $\frac{1}{4}$

He buys a jacket from Top Garms. How much cheaper would it have been to buy the jacket from Smart Togs?

Answer: £ _____

Puzzles 4

Now for a break from 10-minute tests. Try out your skills on these puzzles.

The Scale Factor

An artist is making scale models of two famous buildings. Each model has a different scale factor. Work out the missing values in the diagram below.

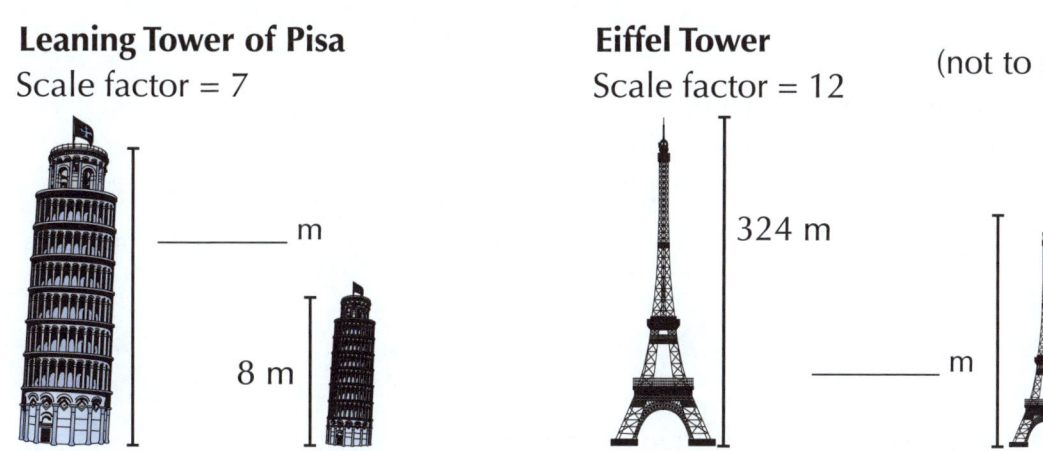

Leaning Tower of Pisa
Scale factor = 7

_____ m

8 m

Eiffel Tower
Scale factor = 12

(not to scale)

324 m

_____ m

How much taller would the artist's Leaning Tower of Pisa model be if they had used a scale factor of 4?

_____ m

Food Glorious Food

In the year 2119, a time traveller has found some tins of 'Roman Red Lentils' buried in the ground. They each have their best before date written in Roman numerals. Write the correct dates in figures under each tin.

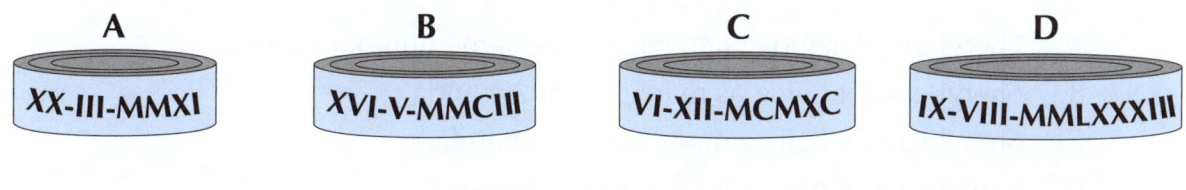

A: XX-III-MMXI
B: XVI-V-MMCIII
C: VI-XII-MCMXC
D: IX-VIII-MMLXXXIII

___-___-___   ___-___-___   ___-___-___   ___-___-___

Which tin of Roman Red Lentils (A-D) went out of date most recently? _____

Test 11

You have **10 minutes** to do this test. Work as quickly and accurately as you can.

1. Eduardo goes to bed at quarter to nine every evening.
   What is this time in the 24-hour format?

   Answer: _____

2. Evelyn has drawn half a shape.
   She then reflects it in the mirror line.
   What is the name of the new shape?

   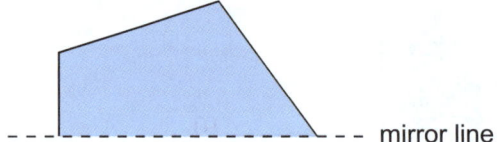

   Answer: _____

3. Linda needs to pay Tom and Brian their wages.
   She's calculated that for every £4 Tom earns, Brian earns £6.
   Linda has £400 to share among them. How much does Brian earn?

   Answer: £ _____

4. Sheryl and Amanda are on their way back from a fishing trip.
   Between them, they caught 23 fish. Which of the following could be correct?
   Circle the correct option.

   A   Sheryl and Amanda each caught the same number of fish.
   B   Sheryl caught twice as many fish as Amanda.
   C   Sheryl caught half as many fish as Amanda.
   D   Sheryl caught one more fish than Amanda.
   E   Sheryl caught 10 times as many fish as Amanda.

5. At the end of her birthday party, Zaynab has ³⁄₄ of a pizza left. She shares it equally between her and her dad. How much of the whole pizza do they each get? Circle the correct option.

    A ⁶⁄₈   **B** ³⁄₇   **E** ³⁄₈
    B ³⁄₅   **C** ¹²⁄₈

6. Alejandro sets off from home on his bike at 11:00 am.
The graph shows how his distance from home changes over time.

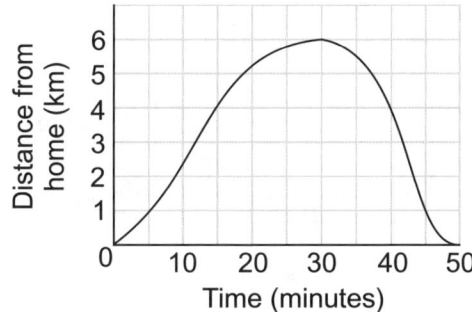

At what time did he turn around and head back towards home?

Answer: _____ am

7. At the start of the month, Alyssa has £410 in her savings. She wants to buy a car costing £1350. At the end of every month, she adds £200 to her savings. How many months will it take until she can afford the car? Circle the correct option.

    A 5 months   **C** 10 months   **E** 14 months
    B 7 months   **D** 12 months

8. ¼ of the phone calls Kai receives are from his mum.
⅓ are from his dad, and the rest are from his girlfriend.
What fraction of the phone calls are from his girlfriend?

Answer: _____

9. Patrice has a storage room, shown below.
She puts a box that has equal side lengths of 2 m in the corner.

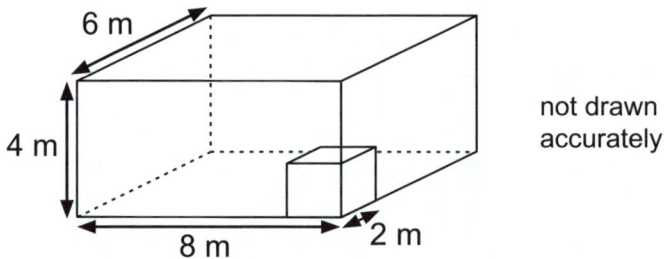

not drawn accurately

What is the volume of the remaining space in the storage room?
Circle the correct option.

A   192 m³   C   200 m³   E   246 m³
B   184 m³   D   162 m³

10. A lasagne recipe uses 500 g of mince and serves four people.
What is the smallest amount of mince needed to make enough
lasagne to serve fourteen people? Circle the correct option.

A   1000 g   C   1500 g   E   2000 g
B   1250 g   D   1750 g

/ 10

Test 11   38   © CGP — not to be photocopied

Test 12

You have **10 minutes** to do this test. Work as quickly and accurately as you can.

1. Dean the fireman can climb a ladder in 17.46 seconds.
   Round this time to 1 decimal place.

   Answer: _____ seconds

2. The table shows the number of different books in Tamsin's home library.

	Fiction	Non-fiction	Total
Hardback	16	28	44
Paperback	39		62
Total	55	51	106

   How many non-fiction paperbacks does she have in her library?

   Answer: _____

3. A teacher wants to buy her pupils some puzzles.
   A jigsaw costs £7.99. How much would 9 jigsaws cost?

   Answer: £ _____

4. At a party, 20% of all the children wore fancy dress.
   What fraction of the children wore fancy dress? Circle the correct option.

   A $\frac{1}{20}$ B $\frac{1}{2}$ C $\frac{1}{4}$ D $\frac{3}{20}$ E $\frac{1}{5}$

5. Philippa has some chocolate bars, each with the following dimensions:

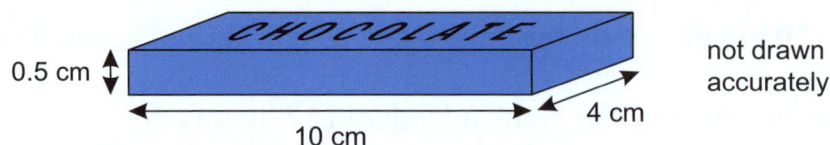

How many chocolate bars can Philippa fit into a box that measures 10 cm × 8 cm × 2 cm? Circle the correct option.

   A 2   B 4   C 5   D 8   E 10

6. The headline for a newspaper story is shown below.

> **Richdale Bring in More Fans than Tottington**
>
> On Saturday, Richdale's brand new 10 000 seat stadium was ¾ full, whereas Tottington's 25 000 seat stadium was only half full.

Which of the following statements is correct? Circle the correct option.

   A   The headline is false — Tottington had 2500 more fans attending.
   B   The headline is true — Richdale had 2500 more fans attending.
   C   The headline is false — Tottington had 5000 more fans attending.
   D   The headline is true — Richdale had 5000 more fans attending.
   E   The headline is false — Tottington had 7500 more fans attending.

7. Mr Mayor is giving a speech at 11:50 am, which lasts for 35 minutes. He is then opening a new town hall at 4:20 pm. How much time is there between the end of his speech and the opening of the town hall? Circle the correct option.

   A   3 hours 25 minutes   D   4 hours 30 minutes
   B   3 hours 40 minutes   E   4 hours 35 minutes
   C   3 hours 55 minutes

8. Three corners of a parallelogram have coordinates: (1, 2), (2, 6) and (6, 6).
    A jewel has been hidden at the fourth corner of the trapezium. At which coordinate is the jewel hidden? Circle the correct option.

    A   (4, 4)
    B   (5, 2)
    C   (6, 2)
    D   (2, 7)
    E   (2, 1)

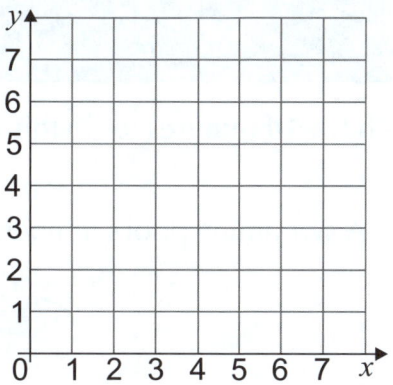

9. Hamish is selling hot dogs. Each hot dog costs him 85p to make and he sells them for £2 each.

    In a day, he sells 43 hot dogs. How much profit does he make?

    Answer: £ _____

10. A zookeeper made a table that shows the number of all the different birds in the zoo.

Type of bird	Number
Parrot	50
Dove	30
Flamingo	100
Vulture	20

    He decides that he wants to make a pie chart to show the different birds in the zoo. What angle would the vulture sector of the pie chart have? Circle the correct option.

    A   20°   B   10°   C   36°   D   90°   E   45°

    / 10

Test 13

You have **10 minutes** to do this test. Work as quickly and accurately as you can.

1. A swimming pool's temperature is measured using a thermometer.

   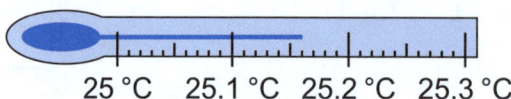

   What is the temperature of the pool?

   Answer: _____ °C

2. Azim's friends want to know how many spinning tops he owns.
   The amount he owns is a prime number, has two digits, and is a factor of 33.
   How many spinning tops does Azim own? Circle the correct option.

   A 99   B 11   C 3   D 33   E 13

3. A group of 66 pupils took a maths test, marked out of 10.
   The results are shown in the bar chart.

   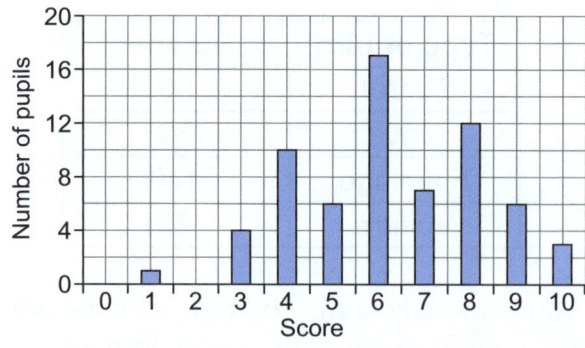

   Anyone who scored 6 or less has to resit the test.
   How many pupils don't have to resit the test?

   Answer: _____

4. Ana buys a 40 m ball of string. She cuts off three pieces, each 120 cm long.
   What length of string is left in the ball? Circle the correct option.

   A   38.8 m   C   4 m   E   42.2 m
   B   34.6 m   D   36.4 m

5. Jerry plays 40 games of snooker and wins 24.
   What percentage of the games that Jerry played did he lose?

   Answer: _____ %

6. A cake factory makes 146 287 cakes a year.
   Circle the best estimate for the number of cakes the factory makes in a week.

   A   500   C   3000   E   20 000
   B   1500   D   5000

7. Five people were asked how many times they had been to the cinema
   in the past year. Four of their answers are shown in the table below.

Name	Cinema Trips
Agneska	9
Boris	7
Carmen	8
Deepak	6
Eleanor	

   The mean answer was 8. How many times did Eleanor go to the cinema?
   Circle the correct option.

   A   8   B   7   C   9   D   10   E   12

8. Dev has two identical tetrahedrons. Both have 4 equal faces, each of area 6 cm². He glues the tetrahedrons together to give the shape shown. He wants to cover the outside of the new shape with coloured paper. What total area of paper does he need? Circle the correct option.

    A   36 cm²   C   72 cm²   E   88 cm²
    B   48 cm²   D   144 cm²

9. A bucket can hold 6 litres of water. The bucket has a crack in it, and it leaks water at a constant rate of 10 ml each hour. Terry fills the bucket to the top at 7:00 am. He returns at 11:30 am. How much water is left in the bucket at this time?

    Answer: _____ ml

10. A builder has drawn up a plan to build a circular pond next to his house.

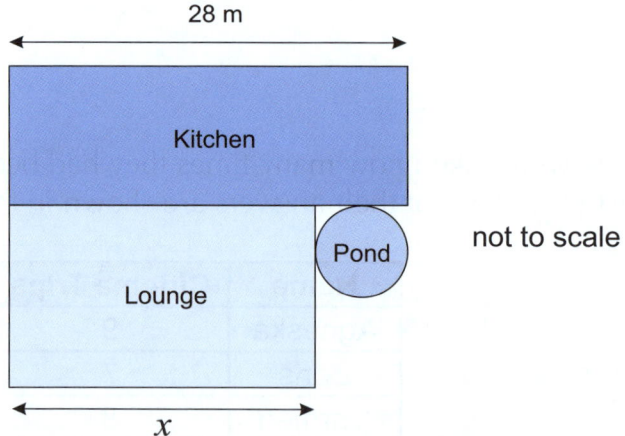

not to scale

He knows that the length of the lounge is exactly ³⁄₄ the length of the kitchen. What is the diameter of the pond in metres?

    Answer: _____ m

/ 10

Test 13   44   © CGP — not to be photocopied

Puzzles 5

Now for a break from 10-minute tests. Try out your skills on this puzzle.

Robert's Reflections

Robert Reflection has been writing secret codes to Molly Mirror using lines drawn on a grid. Part of the code below is missing. Follow Robert's instructions to complete the code, then reflect the code in the *x*-axis to reveal the message.

- Draw a straight line connecting (−7, −1) and (−6, −3).
- Draw a straight line connecting (−6, −3) and (−5, −1).
- Draw a straight line connecting (−7, −2) and (−5, −2).

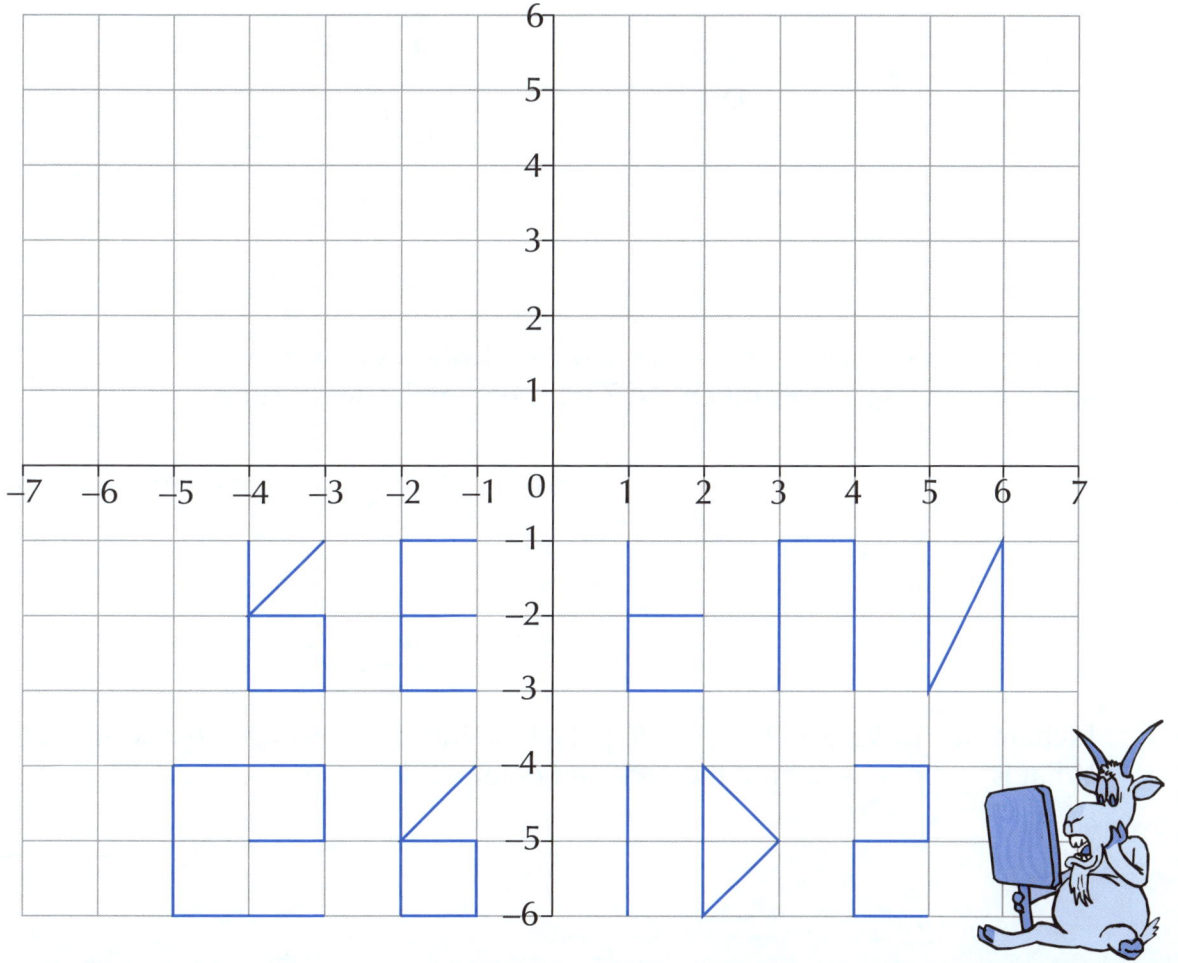

Test 14

You have **10 minutes** to do this test. Work as quickly and accurately as you can.

1. A van has travelled 189 451 miles. Round this figure to the nearest thousand.

    Answer: _____ miles

2. Geraint needs 30 g of chocolate chips to make one cake.
   He has 325 g of chocolate chips. How many cakes can he make?
   Circle the correct option.

    A 9   **C** 11   **E** 13
    B 10   **D** 12

3. Zara went to the sweet shop. She had £3.20 when she went in and left with 74p. How much did Zara spend in the sweet shop?

    Answer: £ _____

4. Richard has 14 kg of potatoes. He puts them into a potato sack that weighs 200 g. What is the total weight of the sack and potatoes, in grams?

    Answer: _____ g

5. Ben draws a regular hexagon, shown below.

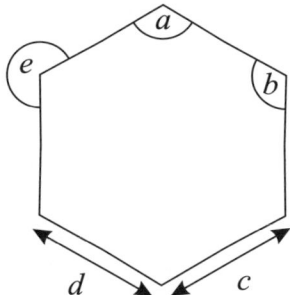

Which of the following statements is true? Circle the correct option.

    A   Angle *a* is larger than angle *b*.
    B   All the interior angles add to up to 360°.
    C   Side *c* is parallel to side *d*.
    D   Sides *c* and *d* have the same length.
    E   Angle *e* is an acute angle.

6. A large bag of dog biscuits costs £6.99. They are on a 'buy one get one free' special offer. Eddie needs six bags for the local animal shelter. How much will this cost, once the special offer has been applied?

Answer: £ _____

7. An author signs a new book deal. The amount in pounds that the author will earn is based on the formula $15p + 25\,000$. *p* is the number of pages in the finished book. How much money will they earn if they write 300 pages?

Answer: £ _____

8. Darius has $2/3$ of a chocolate bar left. He gives $3/4$ of what remains to his friends. What fraction of the entire chocolate bar has Darius given to his friends?

Answer: _____

9. Morgan is at the post office (**P**) and needs to get to the supermarket (**S**). Which of the following would get Morgan to the supermarket from the post office? Circle the correct option.

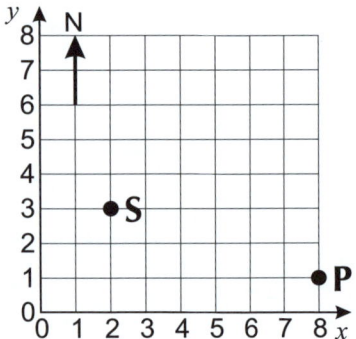

A   6 squares west, 1 square north, 1 square east
B   3 squares north, 6 squares west, 1 square south
C   5 squares west, 2 squares north, 2 squares west
D   1 square south, 3 squares west, 7 squares north
E   2 squares north, 1 square west, 3 squares north

10. A café asked 60 people what their favourite sandwich was. The results are shown in the pie chart to the right. How many people said egg was their favourite? Circle the correct option.

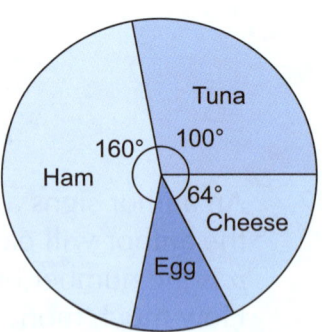

A   36   C   4   E   6
B   10   D   2

Test 15

You have **10 minutes** to do this test. Work as quickly and accurately as you can.

1. Martin drew the following shape. How many lines of symmetry does it have?

   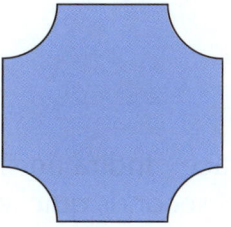

   Answer: _____

2. Scarlet is going on holiday. She says the number of days she will spend on holiday is a square number. Which of the following can't be the number of days Scarlet is spending on holiday? Circle the correct option.

   A   9 days   C   16 days   E   15 days
   B   25 days   D   4 days

3. The bar chart shows the colour of all the front doors along one street of houses.

   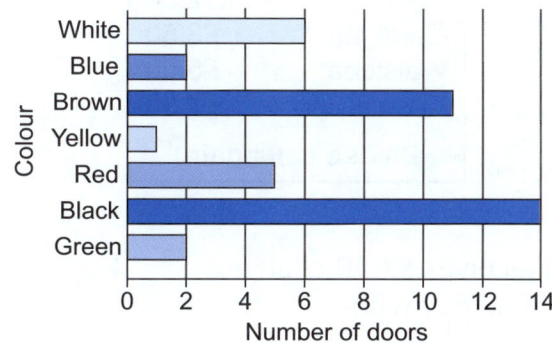

   How many of the houses on the street have a front door with a colour that begins with the letter 'B'?

   Answer: _____

4. Joshua is flying a helicopter at a constant speed. He flies 120 km in one hour. How many metres does he travel each minute? Circle the correct option.

   A   200 m   C   1200 m   E   120 m
   B   2000 m   D   60 m

5. Indira and Zoe run a 1500 m race. Indira finished with a time of 6 minutes 23 seconds. Zoe's time was 28 seconds quicker. What time did Zoe finish in?

   Answer: _____ minutes _____ seconds

6. Greg takes his clothes into the dry cleaners. His receipt is shown below.

   Dry Cleaning
Overcoat	£8.00
Dress suit	£12.50
Cardigan	£3.50
Waistcoat	£5.00
Kilt	£7.50

   Please call again!

   He pays in cash, and receives £3.50 change.
   How much money did he pay with?

   Answer: £ _____

7. Jerrika places marbles to create the sequence shown on the right. For which pattern will Jerrika need to place 25 marbles?

    Pattern 1   Pattern 2   Pattern 3

    Answer: _____

8. The graph shows the average daily temperatures during one week in winter. Why is the graph misleading? Circle the correct option.

    A   One week isn't enough information.
    B   It should show one week in summer too.
    C   −9 °C is too cold.
    D   Friday and Saturday have the same average temperature.
    E   The numbers on the vertical axis go in the wrong direction.

    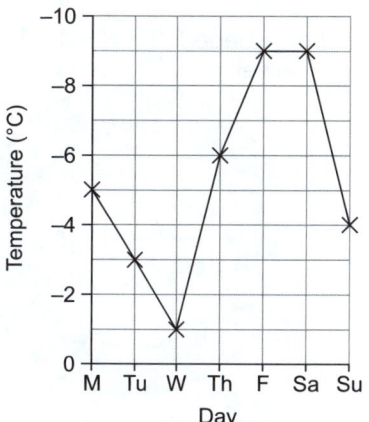

9. Antonia went into a shop with £120. She spent $^3/_8$ of the money on food and $^3/_5$ of the money on furniture. How much money did she leave with?

    Answer: £ _____

10. An average of 20 g of food is taken from Mr Chapman's bird feeder each day. If he starts off with 560 g of food in his feeder, which expression shows how many grams will be left after n days? Circle the correct option.

    A $20n - 560$
    B $(560 \div n) - 20$
    C $560 - 20n$
    D $560 \div 20n$
    E $20n + 560$

/ 10

Puzzles 6

Now for a break from 10-minute tests. Try out your skills on this puzzle.

A Bond of Trust

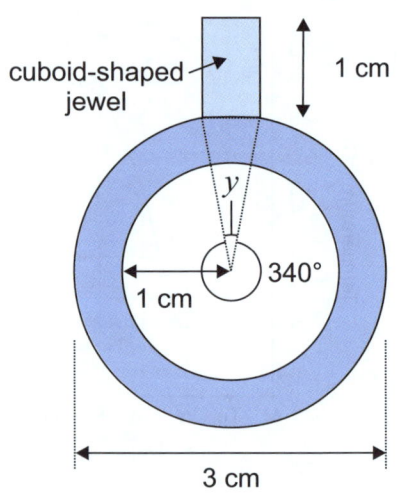

While strolling through a crowded market, Fatima finds a ring on the floor. Five people approach her, each claiming to own the ring.

To help her work out the person who actually owns the ring, Fatima asks each of them to give a fact about the ring.

From the diagram of the ring on the left and the facts below, decide who the ring belongs to.

Michelle: "The diameter of the inside of the ring is exactly $\frac{1}{3}$ of the diameter of the outside of the ring."

Georgia: "The angle y is given by the equation: $12 + 3y = 4y - 8$."

John: "The height from the bottom of the ring to the top of the jewel is 3.5 cm."

Thomas: "The number of faces on the jewel, f, is given by the equation: $2f = f + 24$."

Hassan: "The ring is t cm thick, where t is given by the equation: $2t = 2 - t$."

Who is the ring's rightful owner? _____

Test 16

You have **10 minutes** to do this test. Work as quickly and accurately as you can.

1. Susan and Geoff are waiting for a train. Susan looks at her 24-hour watch and tells Geoff that it is 12:55. Is this am or pm on a 12-hour clock?

    Answer: _____

2. The table shows the heights in metres of 4 pupils in Mr Chu's class.

Name	Len	Sam	Ash	Rod
Height (m)	1.524	1.425	1.568	1.580

    Which of these correctly shows the pupils in order of height, from shortest to tallest? Circle the correct option.

    A   Len, Sam, Ash, Rod
    B   Rod, Ash, Len, Sam
    C   Sam, Ash, Len, Rod
    D   Sam, Len, Ash, Rod
    E   Ash, Len, Rod, Sam

3. Trudy has four different flavours of sweets in a jar.
    She has 47 cola, 56 lemon, 52 cherry and 24 pear.
    How many sweets does she have in the jar altogether?

    Answer: _____

4. A shop is having a sale where everything is reduced by $1/3$ of the original price. A bag originally cost £75. How much does the bag cost in the sale?

    Answer: £ _____

5. Dan is thinking of a number. It is square, a multiple of 9, less than 100, and has 4 as a factor. What number is he thinking of?

Answer: _____

6. The sign below shows the price of different types of fruit at a greengrocers.

Price per kg	
Apples	£2.05
Apricots	£4.05
Cherries	£8.05
Plums	£5.05

Trevor buys 1 kg of apples, 2 kg of apricots and 3 kg of plums. Which option below correctly completes this calculation to find the total cost of Trevor's fruit?

1 × £2 + 2 × £4 + 3 × £5 ____

Circle the correct option.

A + 20p
B + 30p
C + 50p
D – 20p
E – 30p

7. Train A travels 240 miles in the morning and 315 miles in the afternoon. Train B travels 264 miles in the morning and 299 miles in the afternoon. How many more miles does train B travel overall than train A?

Answer: _____ miles

8. A spinner starts on A. It is spun 135° clockwise and lands on B. The spinner is returned to point A. The spinner is spun anticlockwise. What is the smallest angle through which it must be spun to land on B again?

Answer: _____ °

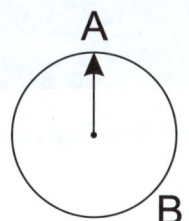

9. Serena drew the following shape on a coordinate grid.

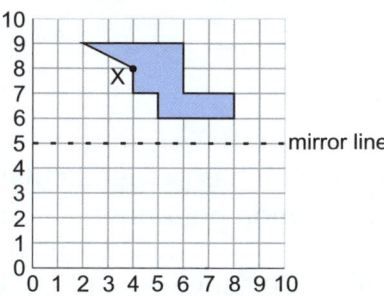

What are the coordinates of point X when Serena reflects the shape in the mirror line? Circle the correct option.

A (4, 2)   **B** (4, 3)   **C** (9, 8)   **D** (4, 8)   **E** (4, 4)

10. Diane makes this sequence of patterns with bricks:

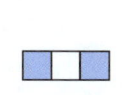   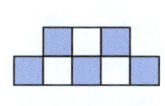   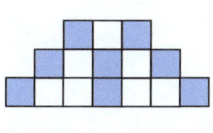   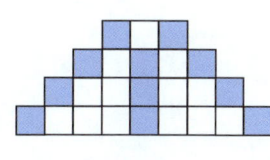

Pattern 1   Pattern 2   Pattern 3   Pattern 4

Circle the expression which shows the number of blue bricks she will use in the nth pattern in the sequence.

A $3n - 1$ **B** $2n + 1$ **C** $2n$ **D** $5n - 7$ **E** $3n$

/ 10

Test 17

You have **10 minutes** to do this test. Work as quickly and accurately as you can.

1. Sanjay says: "The average person breathes around 8 405 912 times each year."
   What does the number 4 represent in this figure? Circle the correct option.

       A   forty million   **C**   four thousand   **E**   four hundred thousand

       B   four million   **D**   forty thousand

2. Linda wants to draw a shape which has perpendicular sides.
   Which of the following should Linda not draw? Circle the correct option.

       A   Square   **C**   Rectangle   **E**   Rhombus

       B   Pentagon   **D**   Triangle

3. Troy has set up a website. Each month the site gets 10 times more visitors than it got the previous month. The site got 54 000 visitors in month four. How many visitors did it get in month one?

   Answer: _____

4. Zola is one of 20 children in her class. The mean number of cousins the children in the class have is 6. What is the total number of cousins the class has?

   Answer: _____

5. A survey is taken to find the average number of miles driven by different professionals in their jobs each year. The results for doctors and police officers are shown in the graph below.

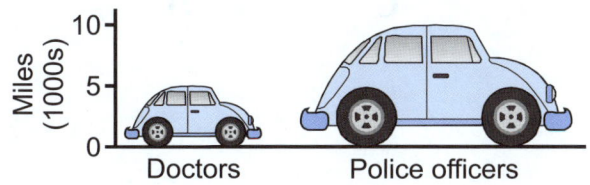

Why is the graph misleading? Circle the correct option.

   A   Not enough numbers are shown on the vertical axis.
   B   It doesn't mention other jobs, like midwives.
   C   The police officers' car is much bigger than the doctors' car.
   D   Doctors don't always have cars in their jobs.
   E   Police cars usually don't look like this.

6. Mr Scarborough asked the other teachers in his school to name their favourite type of music. The chart shows the results.

   What percentage of the teachers said that reggae is their favourite type of music? Circle the correct option.

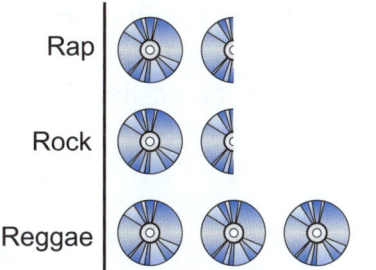

   A   40%   D   75%
   B   20%   E   30%
   C   50%

7. Mrs McIntyre has saved £836 to spend equally on her 11 grandchildren. How much does she spend on each grandchild?

Answer: £ _____

8. Jemma's uncle gives her ¹/₄ of a bag of sweets.
    He gives her friend Fitz ⁴/₅ as many sweets as Jemma.
    What fraction of the bag of sweets does Fitz get? Circle the correct option.

    A   ³/₅   B   ¹/₅   C   ³/₄   D   ¹/₈   E   ¹/₃

9. It takes three robots one hour to clear a field of litter. The robots all work at the same rate. How long would it have taken two robots to clear the field? Circle the correct option.

    A   30 minutes   C   1 hour 15 minutes   E   2 hours
    B   45 minutes   D   1 hour 30 minutes

10. A castle was built in the shape of a 50 m × 30 m rectangle.
    Later, 10 m × 10 m turrets were added. They were centred on each corner of the castle. The diagram shows the castle viewed from above.

    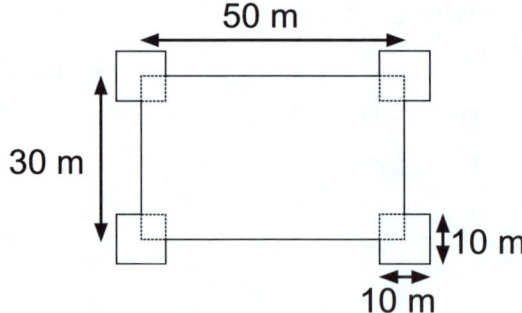

    What is the new perimeter of the castle?

    Answer: _____ m

    / 10

Test 17

Test 18

You have **10 minutes** to do this test. Work as quickly and accurately as you can.

1. Tim is playing a darts game which can be won by throwing a dart into an area that is a multiple of both 2 and 5. Which of the following areas should Tim aim for? Circle the correct option.

   A 15   **B** 6   **C** 20   **D** 18   **E** 1

2. Harry's car was 100 times more expensive than Fay's. Bobby's car was 10 times more expensive than Harry's. Fay paid £255 for her car. How much did Bobby pay for his?

   Answer: £ _____

3. This currency conversion graph can be used to convert pounds (£) to bolivianos.

   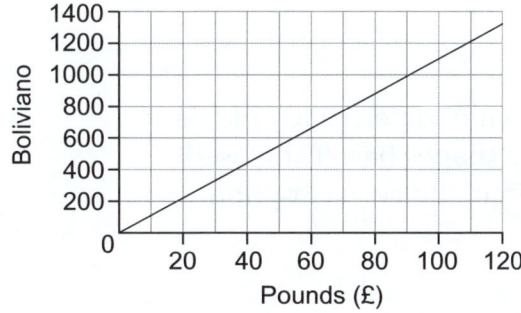

   Approximately how many pounds are equal to 900 bolivianos? Circle the correct option.

   A £82   **C** £1000   **E** £72
   B £105   **D** £120

4. A teacher asked her class to vote whether or not they should have a class pet. 8 pupils said "no", and 17 said "yes". What percentage of the class said "no"?

Answer: _____ %

5. Kimberly buys three bags of sweets, which have a combined mass of 270 g. The three bags have equal mass, and she eats half a bag. How many grams of sweets has she eaten?

Answer: _____ g

6. Andrew's birthday is on 16th June.
Catherine's birthday is 25 days after Andrew's.
What date is Catherine's birthday?

Answer: _____

7. Rhona builds a castle out of different toy blocks. Which of the following shapes hasn't she used to build her castle? Circle the correct option.

    A   Tetrahedron
    B   Cuboid
    C   Triangular prism
    D   Square-based pyramid
    E   Cube

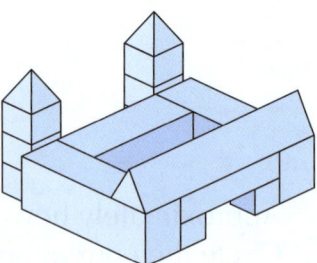

8. Karl thinks of a sequence. To generate each term in his sequence, Karl subtracts three from the previous term, then doubles the result. The sequence starts with 6. What is the eighth term of the sequence?

Answer: _____

9. Karina orders 6 hardback books and 4 paperback books from an online book shop. The prices are shown below.

BOOKS
Hardback   £4.50
Paperback   £2.50
10% discount for any order over £20

How much does Karina's order cost in total?

Answer: £ _____

10. John is rowing across the sea, while Ryan flies a plane above the same route. Ryan travels the same distance in 60 seconds as John does in 1 hour 15 minutes. How long, in hours and minutes, will it take John to travel the same distance as Ryan travels in 10 minutes?

Answer: _____ hour(s) _____ minute(s)

/ 10

Puzzles 7

Now for a break from 10-minute tests. Try out your skills on this puzzle.

Sale Shopping

Anika needs to buy three birthday presents. She goes to her favourite shop, which is having a sale, and spends exactly £40. Work out the sale price of each item, then decide which items she bought.

Shirt

15% off
£20

New price:
_____

Book

50% off
£15

New price:
_____

Scooter

60% off
£60

New price:
_____

Rucksack

25% off
£12

New price:
_____

Necklace

75% off
£28

New price:
_____

Cup

35% off
£10

New price:
_____

Anika bought: _____ , _____ and _____

How much money has Anika saved in the sale? £ _____

Test 19

You have **10 minutes** to do this test. Work as quickly and accurately as you can.

1. A class of pupils were asked where they went on their last holiday. The results are shown in the bar chart to the right. How many pupils are there in the class?

    Answer: _____

    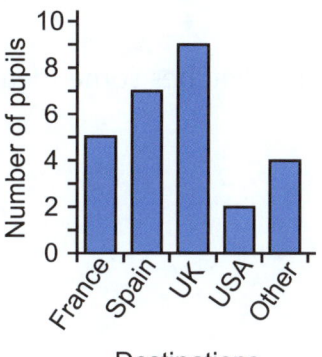
    Destinations

2. Martin joined a slimming club four months ago. In the first month he lost 4.1 kg, in the second month he lost 3.7 kg, in the third month he lost 1.2 kg and in the fourth month he lost 2.2 kg. How much weight has Martin lost in total?

    Answer: _____ kg

3. Alexa writes down a sequence of numbers:

    28, ☐, 10, 1, –8 ...

    What number has she missed out? Circle the correct option.

    A 20   **B** 19   **C** 14   **D** 21   **E** 18

4. Lucy stacks 15 identical dominoes. The height of the stack is 6 cm. How thick is each domino, in millimetres?

    Answer: _____ mm

5. Tara is trying to design a logo out of coloured shapes.
She makes the blue shape below out of a square and an equilateral triangle.

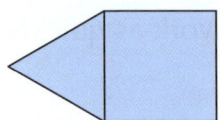

She then sketches some ideas by adding dashed shapes to the logo.

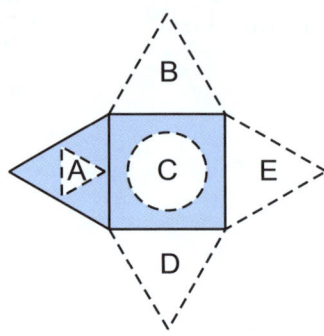

Which shape A-E should she add if she wants to change
how many lines of symmetry the logo has?

Answer: _____

6. Erin has a beaker with 2.5 litres of a chemical in it. She fills some
300 ml flasks with the chemical from the beaker. How many
flasks can she fill completely? Circle the correct option.

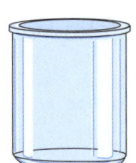

A 15	**C** 7	**E** 4
B 20	**D** 8	

7. Rupert is making bracelets to give to the other 76 pupils in his year group.
He uses 4 beads for each bracelet. He buys a pack of 250 beads.
How many of the 76 pupils will be left without a bracelet?

Answer: _____

8. Mike counts the number of eggs that his chicken lays in one week. The number of eggs is the sum of two square numbers and is also a factor of 15. How many eggs did Mike's chicken lay?

Answer: _____

9. Look at the diagram below.

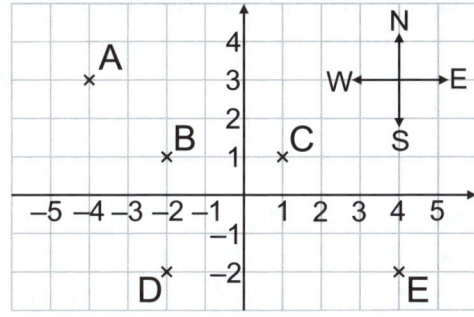

A walker starts at the point (–5, 2). She walks nine units east, four units south, then six units west. At which lettered point is she now standing?

Answer: _____

10. Alpesh arranges matchsticks to create a sequence of patterns. Which formula below gives the number of matchsticks in the nth pattern of this sequence?

 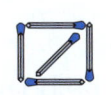 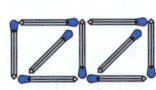 
Pattern 1   Pattern 2   Pattern 3   Pattern 4

Circle the correct option.

A $n + 4$ C $4n + 2$ E $5n - 4$
B $4n - 3$ D $3n + 5$

Test 20

You have **10 minutes** to do this test. Work as quickly and accurately as you can.

1. A geography textbook contains the following information:

   > Japan's coastline is roughly 18 486 miles long.

   What is the length of Japan's coastline rounded to the nearest 100 miles?

   Answer: _____ miles

2. Tracy is taking part in a swim for charity. She is sponsored 50p for every length of the pool she swims. Her target is to raise £50. How many lengths will she have to swim? Circle the correct option.

   A 1000   **B** 25   **C** 100   **D** 200   **E** 10

3. Jack buys 4 ice creams, 4 cold drinks and 2 ice lollies. How much does Jack spend in total?

   Answer: £ _____

Ice Cream Shop	
Ice cream	£1.25
Cold drink	70p
Ice lolly	85p

4. Ethan's teacher has written a list of statements on the board. Ethan knows that only one of the statements is true. Circle the true statement.

   A Multiples of 3 are always odd.
   B A square number can only be divided by itself and 1.
   C Prime numbers are always odd.
   D Multiples of 5 always end in a 5.
   E The sum of three odd numbers is always odd.

5. The pictogram shows the number of people who passed their driving test at a test centre during the first three months of the year.

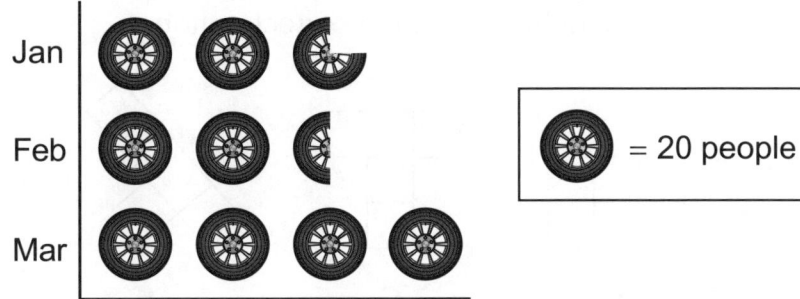

How many more people passed their test in January than in February?

Answer: _____

6. Aslan and his friends are eating a cheese and onion pie. Aslan eats ¼ of the pie and his two friends share the rest equally. What fraction of the whole pie do each of Aslan's friends eat? Circle the correct option.

   A ²/₃   B ³/₄   C ¹/₄   D ³/₈   E ³/₇

7. A plan of Judith's garden is shown below. It is shaped like a trapezium.

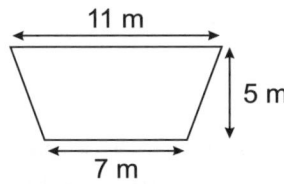

To work out the area of a trapezium, you add together the length of the two parallel sides, halve the result, and multiply it by the height. What is the area of Judith's garden? Circle the correct option.

   A 90 m²   C 45 m²   E 15 m²
   B 55 m²   D 30 m²

8. Aston is creating an open-topped toy box for his children to store all of their toys in. He decides to make a fold-up box using a net. Which of the following nets can't be folded to make an open-topped toy box, as shown on the right? Circle the correct option.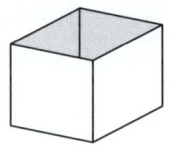

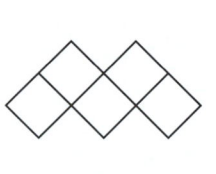 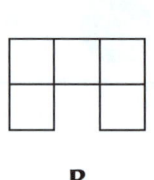 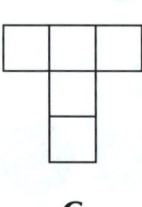 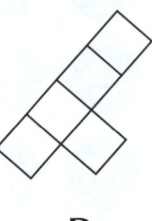 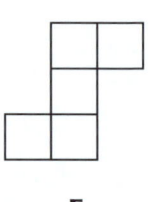

    A   B   C   D   E

9. The table shows the favourite types of films of members of different clubs.

	Sci-Fi	Western	Rom-Com
Swimming Club	7	8	2
Maths Club	1	2	14
Art Club	11	12	1

Which of these statements is false? Circle the correct option.

    A   The most popular type of film overall was Western.
    B   The most popular film type in the Maths Club was Rom-Com.
    C   The Swimming Club has 15 members.
    D   23 members of the Art Club liked either Sci-Fi or Western most.
    E   The Art Club has 7 more members than the Maths Club.

10. Joan makes giant cupcakes. One giant cupcake is shown on the scales. Joan gets an order for 30 giant cupcakes. What is the total weight of the order in kg?

Answer: _____ kg

/ 10

Puzzles 8

Now for a break from 10-minute tests. Try out your skills on these puzzles.

Marble Muddle

Penny had a bag of 150 marbles. 20% of the marbles were red, $3/10$ were blue, one sixth were yellow and the rest were green.

After Penny got home from school, she noticed that some of the marbles were missing. She looked in the bag and could only find 90 marbles.

If all the proportions remain the same, how many marbles of each colour will Penny have lost?

_____ red marbles   _____ blue marbles

_____ yellow marbles _____ green marbles

Flying Fish

Hector and Horace are flying fish. They each have different sized fins. Use the approximate measurements below to estimate the area of their fins.

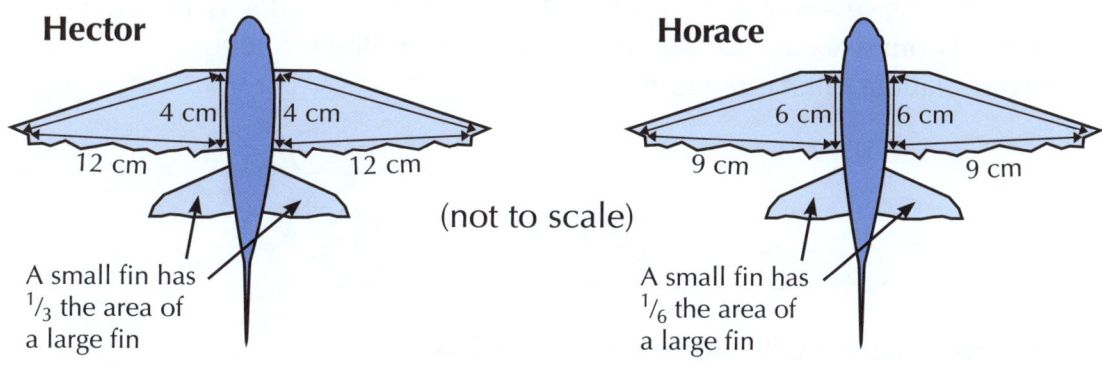

Hector — 4 cm, 4 cm, 12 cm, 12 cm. A small fin has $1/3$ the area of a large fin.

Horace — 6 cm, 6 cm, 9 cm, 9 cm. A small fin has $1/6$ the area of a large fin.

(not to scale)

Which fish has the largest estimated fin area? _____

Test 21

You have **10 minutes** to do this test. Work as quickly and accurately as you can.

1. The temperature in Moscow is –9 °C. The temperature in Sydney is 21 °C. What is the difference in temperature?

   Answer: _____ °C

2. A furniture shop is having a sale where everything is 25% off.

   A settee cost £800 before the sale, but its price tag has been torn. How much does it cost during the sale?

   Answer: £ _____

3. Claudia and Dave are playing a game. Claudia has to put down a certain number of counters each turn until Dave figures out the sequence. Here are Claudia's first three turns:

   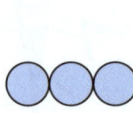 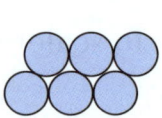 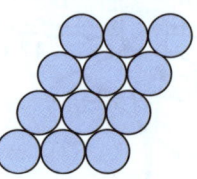

   How many counters will appear on her fourth turn?

   Answer: _____

4. Ellen is at a funfair and is given 5 shapes. To win a prize, Ellen has to pick the shape which has exactly one line of symmetry. Which shape should she pick? Circle the correct option.

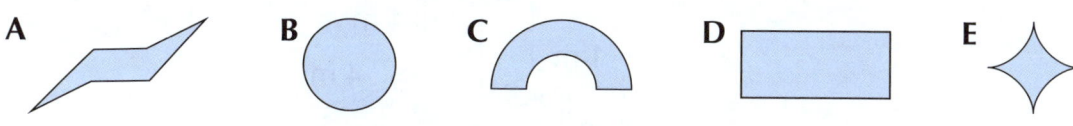

5. Gita was 1.2 m tall on her 10th birthday. Every year for five years she grew 10 cm. How tall was she, in centimetres, on her 15th birthday?

Answer: _____ cm

6. Mr Green is separating 150 kg of sand into buckets. Each bucket can hold 20 kg of sand. How many buckets will he need? Circle the correct option.

    A   8   C   7   E   15
    B   10   D   4

7. Maria is holding a bake sale. She spends £11 on ingredients, and makes 40 cupcakes and 100 biscuits. She sells her cupcakes for £1.50 each and her biscuits for 80p each. How much profit does she make?

Answer: £ _____

8. Two shipping containers are stacked to make the shape below.

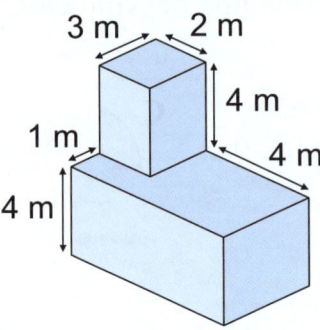

What is the total volume of the shipping containers?

Answer: _____ m³

9. Kirsten uses a sequence to draw lines on a coordinate grid.
She starts at the point (0, 0).
On her first go, she moves one space up and one space to the right.
On her second go, she moves 2 spaces up and 2 spaces to the right.
On her third go, she moves 3 spaces up and 3 spaces to the right.
At what point will she be after her fifth go? Circle the correct option.

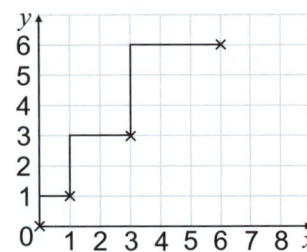

A (5, 5)   D (15, 15)
B (11, 11)   E (16, 16)
C (10, 10)

10. Sam has £350 in his savings account. Each month he saves another £50.
Which expression gives the total amount of money he will have saved in x months time? Circle the correct option.

A $350 \div 50x$ C $350 - 50x$ E $350 + 50x$
B $350x$ D $350 \times 50x$

/ 10

Test 22

You have **10 minutes** to do this test. Work as quickly and accurately as you can.

1. Justine is finding out when some of the trees in her local woods were planted. She writes down the type of tree and the year it was planted.
   Which of the following trees is the youngest? Circle the correct option.

       A Willow — 1931   **C** Ash — 1991   **E** Yew — 1688
       B Oak — 1789   **D** Beech — 1854

2. At an amusement arcade, Eddie changes £4.50 into 50 pence pieces. How many 50 pence pieces does he receive?

   Answer: _____

3. The pictogram below shows how many muffins a bakery sold on each day of the week.

Day	Muffins
Monday	🧁 🧁(half)
Tuesday	
Wednesday	🧁 🧁 🧁 🧁 🧁
Thursday	🧁 🧁
Friday	🧁 🧁 🧁 🧁(half)

   🧁 = 6 muffins

   How many more muffins were sold on Wednesday than on Friday?

   Answer: _____

4. A rectangular piece of cloth measures 35 cm by 42.5 cm. Lucy is sewing a ribbon around the outside edge of the cloth. What length of ribbon does she need?

Answer: _____ cm

5. Jeremy can fit twelve tins of baked beans into one crate.
How many crates will he need to hold 140 tins of beans?
Circle the correct option.

    A   11   **B**   8   **C**   13   **D**   12   **E**   10

6. Ted is talking to the other farmers about his pigs.
He gives them clues about the number of pigs he has:

- The number is a prime number between 20 and 50.
- The number is 2 less than a square number.
- The sum of the number's digits equals a prime number less than 10.

How many pigs does Ted have?

Answer: _____

7. Sergei and Dan are eating a pork pie.
Sergei eats $\frac{1}{4}$ of the pie and Dan eats $\frac{3}{8}$ of the pie.
How much of the pie is left over? Circle the correct option.

    A $\frac{3}{8}$ **B** $\frac{1}{4}$ **C** $\frac{1}{2}$ **D** $\frac{1}{8}$ **E** $\frac{1}{12}$

8. A class is asked to name their favourite colour. The results are shown in the bar chart below. Why is this bar chart misleading? Circle the correct option.

   A   The bars are the wrong colours.
   B   There are no bars for 5 and 6.
   C   Not all colours are listed.
   D   Each bar should represent a colour, not a number.
   E   The numbers should start from 0.

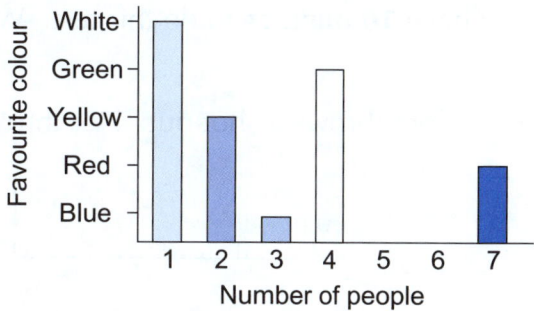

9. A biscuit barrel contains ginger biscuits and chocolate biscuits. There are 44 biscuits in total, and there are 20 more ginger biscuits than chocolate biscuits. How many ginger biscuits does the barrel contain?

   Answer: _____

10. An isosceles triangle is joined to a rectangle to create a wooden fence panel for a rose garden, as shown. One hundred of the fence panels are joined side-by-side to create the fence. What area of wood is needed to create the fence? Circle the correct option.

   A   65 000 cm²   D   95 500 cm²
   B   75 000 cm²   E   44 100 cm²
   C   88 200 cm²

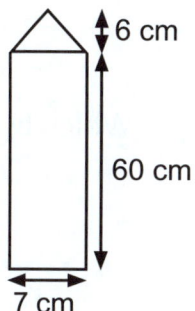

not drawn accurately

Test 23

You have **10 minutes** to do this test. Work as quickly and accurately as you can.

1. Flora throws a shot put. Her throw is measured using the measuring line below.

   The arrow shows where the shot put landed.
   How far did she throw the shot put?

   Answer: _____ m

2. James counts the number of vehicles he sees on the road to work.
   He puts the data in a pie chart.

   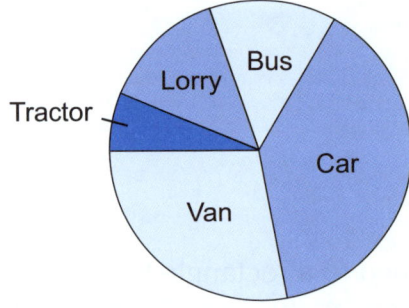

   Which two types of vehicle did he see the same number of?

   Answer: _____ and _____

3. A newborn puppy measures 10 cm from nose to tail.
   When it is fully-grown it is twelve times this length.
   How long is the fully-grown dog in metres?

   Answer: _____ m

4. A teacher places some 2D shapes onto the floor and then puts two rings over them to create the Venn diagram below.

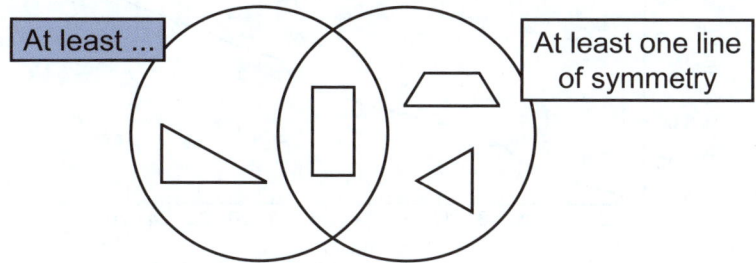

The teacher asks the class how they might label the left ring.
Which of the options below could they use to complete the shaded label?
Circle the correct option.

    A ... one right angle   **D** ... three sides

    B ... one pair of parallel lines   **E** ... one obtuse angle

    C ... one pair of equal sides

5. Jesse buys one of everything on the menu shown. He gets 65p change. How much money did he pay with? Circle the correct option.

Bacon Roll	£2.20
Meat Pie	£1.80
Steak Pudding	£1.65
Sausage Pasty	£1.70

    A £10   **C** £8   **E** £7

    B £5   **D** £20

6. A train takes 27 minutes to get from Oak Green to Central Station. It arrives at Central Station at 14:12. What time did it leave Oak Green? Circle the correct option.

    A 14:39   **C** 02:39   **E** 13:55

    B 01:45   **D** 13:45

7. Andrei completed a 500 km row down a river for charity.
His progress is shown in the line graph below.

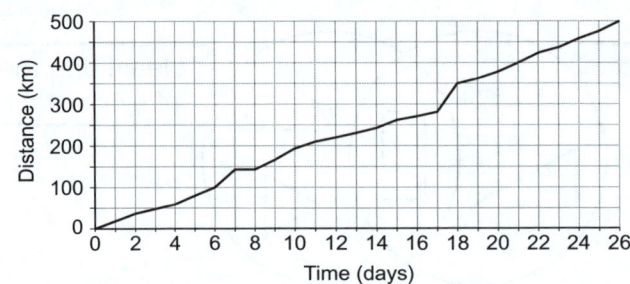

If Andrei started just after midnight on Monday,
what day was it when he'd rowed 250 km?

Answer: _____

8. A recipe for meatballs uses 4 parts beef for every 3 parts pork.
Madison has 2 kg of beef. How many grams of pork will she need?

Answer: _____ g

9. An unloaded lorry has a mass of 6000 kg. A crate of car parts has a mass of
2000 kg. A bridge can support a total mass of 21 000 kg. How many full
crates of car parts can the lorry transport across the bridge in one journey?

Answer: _____

10. Eliza is buying red and yellow tiles to make a mosaic. She uses the formula
$8r + 50$ to work out how many yellow tiles she needs if she buys r red tiles.
How many yellow tiles will she need if she buys 70 red tiles?
Circle the correct option.

A 560   C 510   E 570
B 610   D 690

Puzzles 9

Now for a break from 10-minute tests. Try out your skills on these puzzles.

Floorplan Problem

Mrs Butterworth is having a new house built. Below is a floorplan of the ground floor before any of the rooms have been added. There will be a living room, a kitchen, a dining room, a bathroom and a garage.

Complete the floorplan by adding these five rooms. Make sure that you consider all of Mrs Butterworth's requirements. There cannot be any unused space.

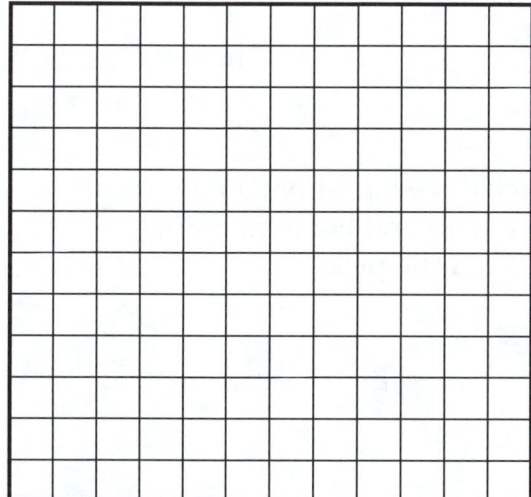

Front door

List of requirements:
1. The living room is the first room you enter when you walk into the house.
2. The kitchen should be $\frac{1}{2}$ the size of the living room.
3. The garage should be the same size as the kitchen.
4. The bathroom should be $\frac{1}{4}$ the size of the living room.
5. The dining room should be $\frac{3}{4}$ the size of the living room.

One to Seven

Place the numbers 1 to 7 in the circles on the right so that each different coloured line adds up to the same number.

You can only use each number once.

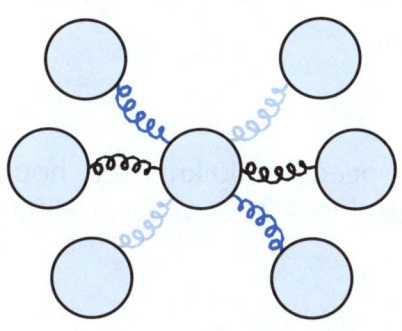

Test 24

You have **10 minutes** to do this test. Work as quickly and accurately as you can.

1. Kayleigh needs to round 14 792 to the nearest thousand.
   What number should she end up with? Circle the correct option.

   A 14 800   C 14 000   E 20 000
   B 15 000   D 10 000

2. A company organises a weekly lottery for all of its workers.
   If nobody wins the prize one week, £25 is added to the total
   prize. After 3 weeks, nobody has won the prize, which now
   stands at £175. How much money was the prize to start with?

   Answer: £ _____

3. At a fair, Andrea plays a game where you pick three balls from a pot
   and add up the numbers. Andrea picks three balls and her total is 60.
   From the 6 balls shown below, which 3 balls did she pick?

   Circle the correct option.

   A 34, 23 and 9   D 40, 9 and 17
   B 34, 25 and 17   E 40, 23 and 25
   C 9, 17 and 34

4. A train travels at a speed of 100 km every hour.
   How many minutes does it take to travel 350 km?

   Answer: _____ minutes

5. Jennifer is hosting a party for 10 children and 4 adults. She pours 250 ml of lemonade for each child and 400 ml of lemonade for each adult. The lemonade comes in 2 litre bottles. How many of lemonade bottles does she need to buy?

Answer: _____

6. The timetable shows the TV programmes shown between 6:00 pm and 7:30 pm one night on two channels, CGP 1 and CGP 2.

Start Time	CGP 1	CGP 2
6:00 pm		Athletics
6:15 pm	News	Canoeing
6:30 pm		Swimming
6:45 pm	Weather	
7:00 pm	Food Show	Acrobatics
7:15 pm		Croquet

José watches the News, Weather and Acrobatics. How long does he watch TV for?

Answer: _____ hour(s) _____ minute(s)

7. Jodie wants to put $2/5$ of her clothes into storage. She splits the clothes equally between 4 boxes. What fraction of her clothes will she put into each box? Circle the correct option.

A $2/5$ C $1/10$ E $1/20$
B $2/9$ D $1/4$

8. Jonah leaves his house at 09:00 one day.
He goes to meet a friend, before returning home by 15:00.
His distance from home is shown in the graph below.
How far did he travel between 11:00 and 13:30? Circle the correct option.

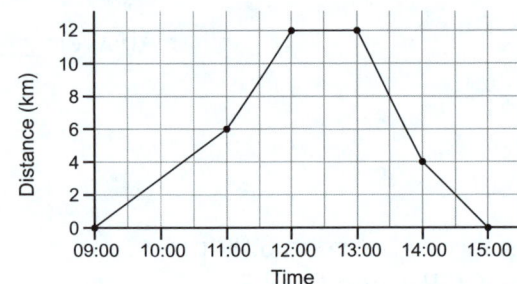

A   22 km
B   12 km
C   26 km
D   10 km
E   6 km

9. Sharon is parking at a car park where the price is £1.10 for each hour of parking. If Sharon stays for x hours, how much does she pay in pence?
Circle the correct option.

A $110x$ C $1.1x$ E $110 + x$
B $110 + 1.1x$ D $110 \times 1.1x$

10. Marjan is making a paper flower. He places a regular hexagon and two regular pentagons all with the same side length together, as shown below.

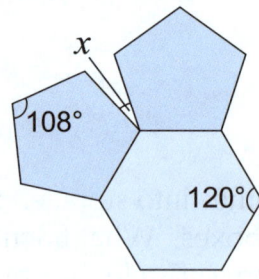

What is the size of angle x?

Answer: _____ °

Test 24   82   © CGP — not to be photocopied

Test 25

You have **10 minutes** to do this test. Work as quickly and accurately as you can.

1. Hatty has twelve cats. Half of them are black, a quarter of them are white and the rest are grey. What fraction of the cats are grey? Circle the correct option.

   A 1/4   **C** 3/7   **E** 1/12
   B 1/6   **D** 1/2

2. Leon is thinking of a shape. He says, "It has four sides. It has two obtuse angles and two acute angles." Which two of the following could he be thinking of?

   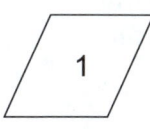   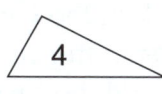

   Circle the correct option.

   A 1 and 2   **C** 3 and 4   **E** 3 and 5
   B 2 and 5   **D** 1 and 3

3. Kate saves money by putting any spare change she has in a jar. On average, she saves £1.50 per week. She currently has £30 in the jar. How many weeks has she been saving for? Circle the correct option.

   A 22   **B** 20   **C** 32   **D** 36   **E** 42

4. A group of children were asked how many pens they have in their pencil case. The results are shown in the bar chart.

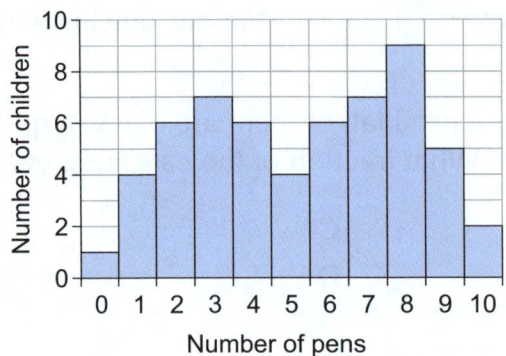

How many children have 6 or more pens in their pencil case?

Answer: _____

5. Parking in a car park costs 50p an hour. Alternatively, a parking permit lets you park in the car park for as long as you want for £250 per year. Harish parks in the car park for 2 hours a day, 275 days a year. How much will he save per year if he buys the parking permit instead of paying by the hour? Circle the correct option.

   A   £75   B   £40   C   £50   D   £45   E   £25

6. Tim records the temperature every hour for five hours.

Time	Temperature
11:00	8 °C
12:00	9 °C
13:00	11 °C
14:00	13 °C
15:00	9 °C

What is the mean of the temperatures he recorded?

Answer: _____ °C

7. A car wheel has a circumference of 150 cm.
How many complete turns would the wheel make if the car travelled 300 m?

Answer: _____

8. Cledwyn has one set of 5 cm-high wooden blocks, and one set of 8 cm-high wooden blocks. He starts stacking them to make two separate towers, as shown. He stops when the two towers are the same height. What is the minimum height that the towers could be at this point?

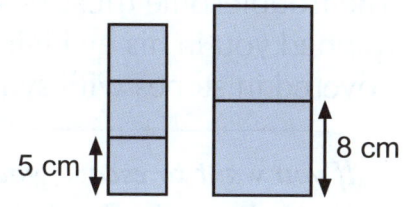

Answer: _____ cm

9. A 330 ml can of pop contains 49.5 ml of fruit juice.
What percentage of the can is fruit juice? Circle the correct option.

A   10%   B   49.5%   C   15%   D   20%   E   33%

10. Henry has a toy Egyptian pyramid. The volume of a square-based pyramid is $\frac{1}{3}$ × area of the base × height. The volume is 4 cm³ and the height is 3 cm. What is the side length of the base of the pyramid?

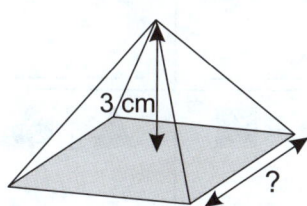

Answer: _____ cm

/ 10

Puzzles 10

Now for a break from 10-minute tests. Try out your skills on this puzzle.

Trapped By a Trickster

The troublesome trickster, Rex Claws, has trapped you in his evil lair. The floor of the lair is covered in stones with symbols written on them.

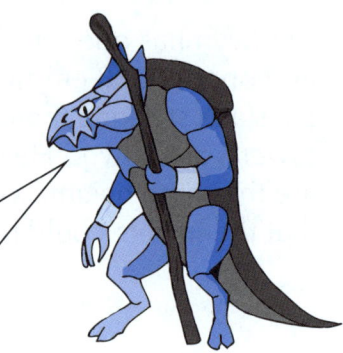

If you want to escape, you'll have to find the path that adds up to 0. You can only step on one stone from each column, and each stone in your path must share an edge or touch at the corner, so choose wisely!

Rex has given you a piece of paper with four clues to solving the puzzle. Use these clues to work out the answer to each calculation, then colour in the four stones you will use to escape.

◆ = the number of sides on 3 pentagons

♣ = the number of hours in 480 minutes

▲ = the difference between LXX and C

■ = the number 24 000 divided by 1000

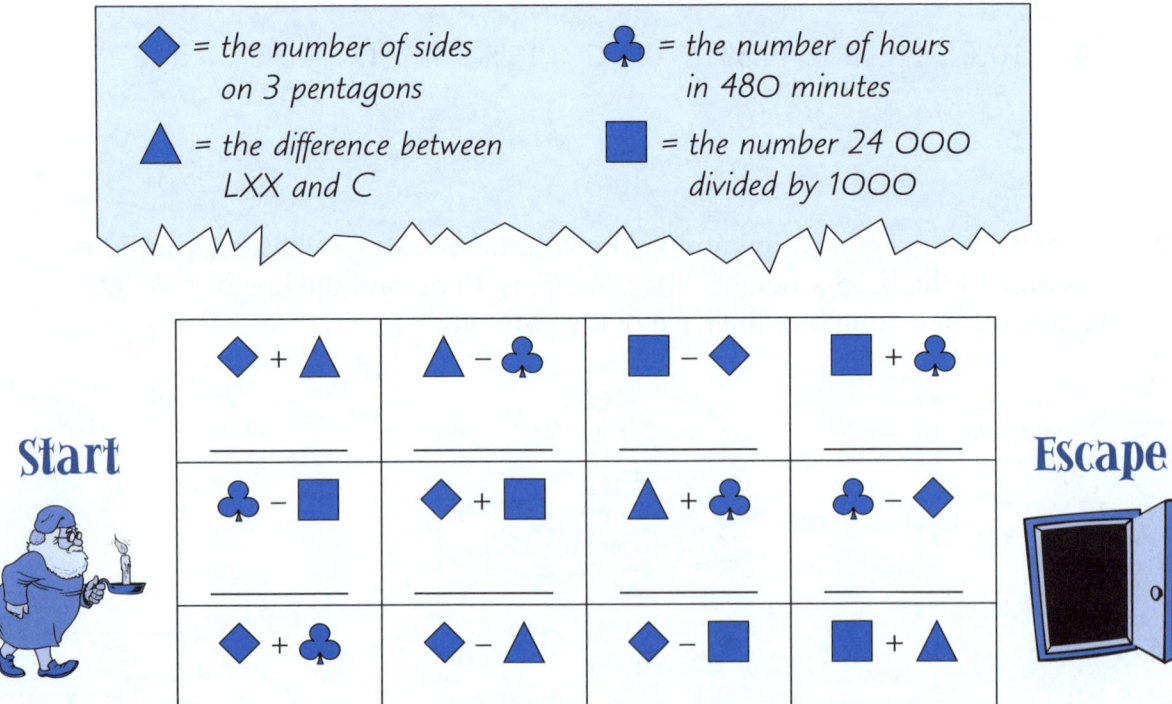

Test 26

You have **10 minutes** to do this test. Work as quickly and accurately as you can.

1. The table shows the final leader board for a race. One of the times is missing.

Position	Name	Time (seconds)
1st	Bernard	18.650
2nd	Oscar	19.025
3rd	Raymond	?
4th	Jackson	19.134

   Which of these could be Raymond's finishing time, in seconds?
   Circle the correct option.

   A 19.010   C 19.123   E 19.150
   B 19.205   D 19.000

2. Nathan buys some new rugby boots for £36.99, some shorts for £10.29 and some socks for £3.50. How much does he spend in total? Circle the correct option.

   A £50.79   C £50.88   E £60.89
   B £50.78   D £49.78

3. A zookeeper is taking the measurements of different giraffes in an enclosure. He records the length of each giraffe's neck in the following bar chart.

   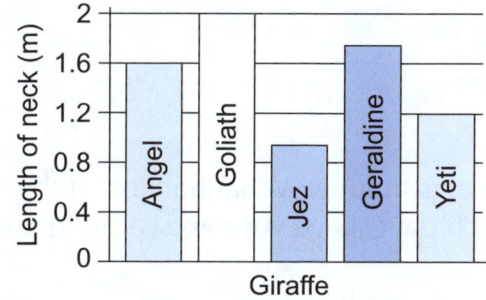

   How much longer is Goliath's neck than Yeti's?

   Answer: _____ m

4. A scientist is observing the number of bacteria in a dish. The table shows the data she records. How many bacteria will there be in the dish after 80 minutes?

Time (minutes)	0	20	40	60	80
Number of bacteria	10	20	40	80	?

Answer: _____

5. 600 litres of water flows over a waterfall in 3 seconds. How much water will flow over the waterfall in 21 seconds?

Answer: _____ litres

6. Look at the biscuit mix ingredients shown below.

Packet Biscuit Mix
Ingredients:
280 g plain flour
60 g golden caster sugar
40 g light brown sugar
20 g dark brown sugar

What percentage of the mix is made up of sugar?

Answer: _____ %

7. Eliza eats $3/4$ of a jar of sweets in June. What fraction of the jar will she have eaten on average each day? Give your answer in its simplest form.

Answer: _____

8. Sharon, Kara and Ryan all catch the train at 5:55 pm. Kara gets off after 35 minutes. Ryan gets off 15 minutes before Kara, and Sharon gets off 10 minutes after Ryan. Which of the following statements is true? Circle the correct option.

    A   Sharon gets off the train at 6:20 pm.
    B   Ryan gets off the train at 6:15 pm.
    C   Sharon gets off the train after Kara.
    D   Sharon spends 1 hour on the train.
    E   Kara gets off the train 5 minutes before Sharon.

9. Remi is sailing from Portsmouth to New York. The route that she is taking is exactly 6076 km. She is 40 miles away from New York. If 8 km is approximately 5 miles, how far has she sailed up to this point? Circle the correct option.

    A   6996 km   C   6012 km   E   6041 km
    B   5012 km   D   6051 km

10. Craig is making a mosaic. He has triangular tiles with a height of 25 mm and a width of 40 mm.

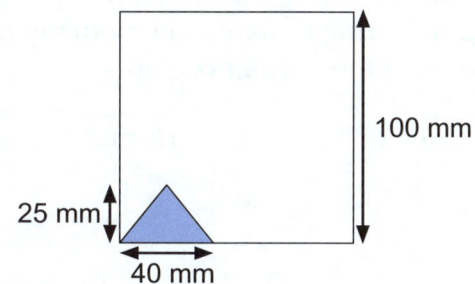

How many whole tiles can he fit on a square board with a width of 100 mm? Circle the correct option.

    A   8   C   12   E   10
    B   20   D   16

/ 10

Test 27

You have **10 minutes** to do this test. Work as quickly and accurately as you can.

1. Katherine buys a computer game for £17.03.
   What is the cost to the nearest 10p?

   Answer: £ _____

2. A box of chocolates contains 15 chocolates.
   Dwayne shares 3 boxes of chocolates equally between himself and 8 friends.
   How many chocolates do they each get?

   Answer: _____

3. For an art project, Simon is making a cube with edges of length 2 m.
   Each edge is made from a string of lights. How many metres of
   lights does he need? Circle the correct option.

   A 8 m   **B** 12 m   **C** 16 m   **D** 18 m   **E** 24 m

4. A daily bus ticket costs £2.45. Suzie buys 5 of these tickets each week.
   How much does this cost her? Circle the correct option.

   A £9.80   **B** £10.45   **C** £12   **D** £12.25   **E** £12.50

5. Tracy records the number of various coins she has in her money box.

Coin	50p	20p	10p	5p	2p	1p
Number of coins	2	4	8	4	10	15

    How much money does she have in her money box in total?

    Answer: £ _____

6. Wendy went on a wildlife-spotting holiday.
    She drew a bar chart to record the number of penguins she saw each day.

    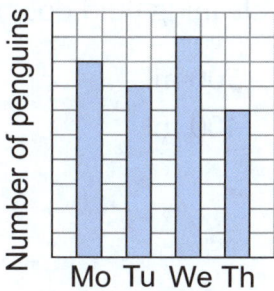

    On Monday, she saw 8 penguins. What is the mean number of penguins she saw each day during her holiday?

    Answer: _____

7. In a game show, a group of 32 people were asked to choose either envelope A, B or C. Half of the people chose envelope C. Four more people chose envelope B than envelope A. How many people chose envelope A?

    Answer: _____

8. Joe is making ice cream. At 7:55 pm on Saturday he leaves it to set.
    The recipe says to leave it 14 hours 30 minutes to set.
    What is the earliest time on Sunday that Joe could eat it?
    Give your answer in the 12-hour clock format.

    Answer: _____

9. Fiona buys a 2 litre bottle of concentrated cleaning fluid. The fluid needs to be diluted with water before use. The instructions on the bottle say to dilute every 100 ml of fluid with 400 ml of water. She mixes some of the fluid with water to fill a 1.5 litre bucket. How much cleaning fluid does she use? Circle the correct option.

    A   375 ml   C   500 ml   E   1200 ml
    B   300 ml   D   400 ml

10. A group of friends are playing a card game. Each player must start with the same number of cards as everyone else, and everyone must have at least 2 cards. All of the cards in the pack are handed out. Which of the following cannot be the number of cards in the pack? Circle the correct option.

    A   32   B   27   C   29   D   21   E   33

/ 10

Test 27

Test 28

You have **10 minutes** to do this test. Work as quickly and accurately as you can.

1. A bag of oranges weighs 475.2 g. Usain has an old set of scales that can only measure a mass to the nearest 10 g. What would the reading for the bag of oranges be on Usain's scales?

   Answer: _____ g

2. At a quiz, a team scored 18 points out of 72. What is this as a fraction in its simplest form?

   Answer: _____

3. A librarian is sorting through all of the books on a library shelf. She counts the number of books in each genre and records the information in a pictogram.

   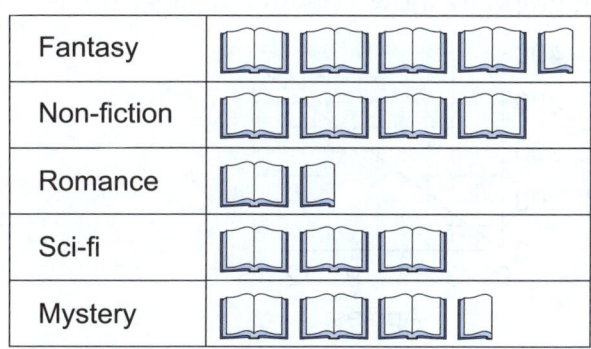

   She removes all the non-fiction books from the shelf. How many books are left on the shelf?

   Answer: _____

4. A tile in the shape of a regular octagon has a side length of 5 cm.
    Eight tiles are arranged in the pattern shown below.

    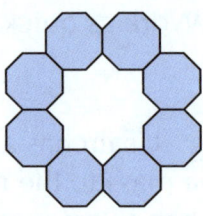

    What is the perimeter of the star shape in the middle? Circle the correct option.

    A   120 cm   C   40 cm   E   400 cm
    B   160 cm   D   80 cm

5. A large box of fudge contains 24 pieces and costs £5.
    A small box of fudge contains 6 pieces and costs £2.
    What is the maximum number of pieces you could buy with £14?

                                                            Answer: _____

6. Antoine wants to make some apple pie filling using his grandma's recipe.
    She gives him the following graph to show how much sugar he needs per apple.

    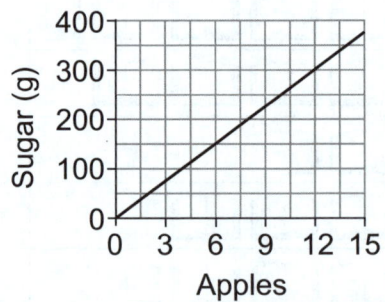

    Antoine has 8 apples. How much sugar, in grams, would he need
    to make as much pie filling possible? Circle the correct option.

    A   120 g   C   180 g   E   225 g
    B   150 g   D   200 g

7. Jayden is 13 years older than his cousin, Jake. Their combined age is 45. How old is Jake? Circle the correct option.

   A 29   B 16   C 18   D 21   E 32

8. Equilateral triangles are placed together to form a path in the shape of a larger equilateral triangle. Each side of the path is made of nine triangles, as partially shown in the diagram below.

   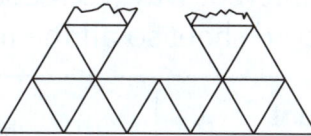

   How many triangles are needed to make the whole path? Circle the correct option.

   A 22   B 27   C 21   D 30   E 33

9. In a survey, 4 in every 15 people said that their favourite festive food was Brussels sprouts. 285 people were surveyed. How many people said that their favourite festive food was Brussels sprouts? Circle the correct option.

   A 57   C 60   E 66
   B 75   D 76

10. Graham's watch is 25 minutes fast. It suddenly stops working. At 17:10, Graham notices, and works out that the watch must have stopped 1 hour 20 minutes ago. What time is shown on Graham's watch? Give your answer in the 24-hour clock format.

    Answer: _____

Puzzles 11

Now for a break from 10-minute tests. Try out your skills on these puzzles.

Conversion Confusion

The members of a dance class are taking part in a competition. Mr Waltz, their teacher, has recorded how long they have spent practising their routines. He's made a mistake and used different ways to record the different times. Fill in the gaps in Mr Waltz's record sheet so all the times are in hours and minutes.

Names	Time spent	Time spent (hours and minutes)
Rania & Mark	237 minutes	
Tom & Bea	From 10:30 am to 4:00 pm (with 30 minutes for lunch)	
Mollie & Sajid	$\frac{2}{3}$ of 9 hours	
Kurt & Shirley	Three 90-minute sessions	

Mr Waltz will award a prize to the couple who spent the most time practising. Which couple will it be?

_____

Find the Prize

On a game show, a star prize is hidden in one of six boxes, as shown below. Using these clues, circle which box holds the star prize.

The star prize...
- ... isn't in a box with a prime number on it.
- ... is in a box with a multiple of 9 on it.
- ... isn't in a box with a square number on it.

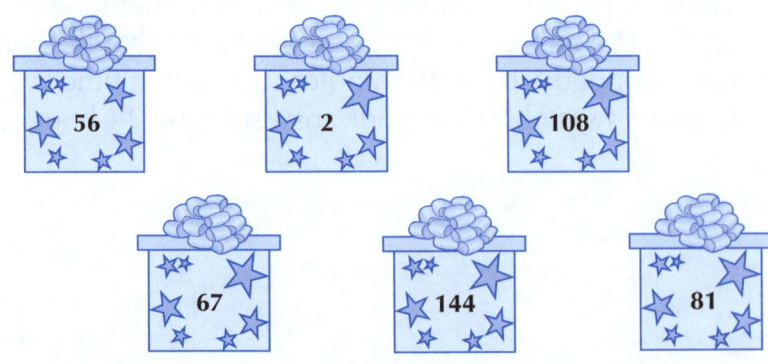

Test 29

You have **10 minutes** to do this test. Work as quickly and accurately as you can.

1. There are 100 paperclips in a packet, and 10 packets in a box. Lloyd orders 13 boxes of paperclips for his office. How many paperclips is this altogether?

    Answer: _____

2. $^3/_5$ of Gemma's toys are cuddly toys. What is this written as a percentage?

    Answer: _____ %

3. Phoebe needs 1.7 m of fabric to make her curtains. Each metre of fabric costs £7.10. How much will the fabric cost her in total? Circle the correct option.

    A £12.07   C £1.21   E £1207
    B £120.70 D £0.12

4. A sack of compost weighs 4.5 kg, and a bag of potatoes weighs 1.5 kg. Six bags of potatoes are placed on one side of a set of scales. The scales will balance only if the weights on each side are equal. How many sacks of compost need to be placed on the other side for the scales to balance perfectly? Circle the correct option.

    A 1   B 2   C 3   D 4   E 5

5. When cooking rice, Gordon uses 200 ml of water for every 100 g of rice.
   How many litres of water does Gordon need if he's cooking 1.5 kg of rice?

   Answer: _____ litres

6. Letisha has 4 playing cards, each with a different number on it.
   She tells her friends that the mean of the numbers on the playing cards is 5.
   She adds another card, then tells her friends that the mean is now 6.
   What number was on the card she added?

   Answer: _____

7. Look at the nutritional information shown below, taken from a packet of biltong.

	Per 100 g
Protein	60 g
Carbohydrate	15 g
(of which sugars)	2 g
Fat	5 g

   The packet contains 250 g of biltong. How many packets of biltong would be needed to provide 300 g of protein? Circle the correct option.

   A 2   B 3   C 4   D 5   E 6

8. Lewis has a field that is 100 m × 100 m. He plants trees 10 m apart, in a grid pattern. The outer trees are planted 10 m from the edge of the field, as shown in the diagram below.

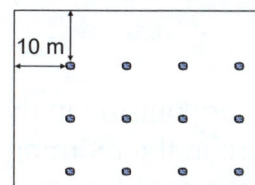

How many trees has Lewis planted? Circle the correct option.

   A   100   B   90   C   81   D   64   E   63

9. Two clocks are shown — one at eight o'clock and one at quarter past eight.

What angle does the hour hand move through between these two times? Circle the correct option.

   A   15°   B   30°   C   7.5°   D   90°   E   22.5°

10. A toy block is a cuboid with sides 1 cm × 2 cm × 4 cm. 240 of these blocks can be neatly stacked in the toy box below to fill it completely.

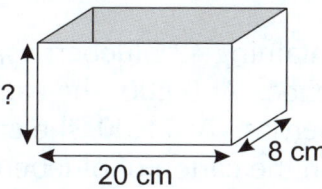

What is the height of the toy box?

Answer: _____ cm

Test 30

You have **10 minutes** to do this test. Work as quickly and accurately as you can.

1. Francesco records the temperature outside in the evening and it is 2 °C.
   He then records the temperature in the morning and it is 4.5 °C colder.
   What temperature is it in the morning?

   Answer: _____ °C

2. A group of 100 people equally share some money won on the lottery. Each person receives £346.47. How much did the group win in total? Circle the correct option.

   A £3.46   C £3464.70   E £346 470
   B £34.64   D £34 647

3. Chantelle has a carton containing 42 blueberries. She eats blueberries from the carton in a sequence. At 09:00, she eats 2 blueberries. At 10:00, she eats 4 blueberries. At 11:00, she eats 6 blueberries. At what time will she finish the carton of blueberries? Circle the correct option.

   A 14:00   B 12:00   C 13:00   D 16:00   E 15:00

4. Mika is thinking of a shape. She says there are 3 different sizes of interior angles. Which of these shapes could she be thinking of? Circle the correct option.

    A Kite   **C** Equilateral triangle   **E** Rhombus
    B Parallelogram   **D** Isosceles triangle

5. The distance-time graph below shows part of a hiker's walk.

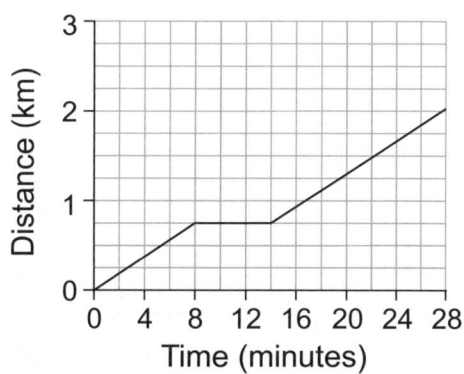

When she is 1.75 km from her starting point, she reaches a field.
After how many minutes does she reach the field?

Answer: _____ minutes

6. Esteban buys a box of hazelnut chocolates and a box of orange chocolates.
He empties the boxes and sorts all of the chocolates into groups.
Each group contains 2 hazelnut chocolates and 5 orange chocolates.
There are 14 hazelnut chocolates altogether.
How many orange chocolates are there altogether?

Answer: _____

7. A field in the shape of a regular pentagon has a perimeter of 550 m. It has a fence around the edge, with each fence panel being 10 m wide. How many fence panels are there on each of the field's sides? Circle the correct option.

   A 5   **B** 7   **C** 10   **D** 11   **E** 55

8. Brendan buys three shirts for £24.59 each and one pair of trousers for £39.65. How much does he spend in total?

   Answer: £ _____

9. A man is making a trail of sand. He is carrying a 15 kg sandbag with a hole that pours out 150 g of sand for every 100 m he walks. How long will the trail be, in km, by the time the sandbag is empty?

   Answer: _____ km

10. A café asks 40 people what their favourite type of coffee is. 22 people say cappuccino. The results are plotted on a pie chart. What angle will the cappuccino sector of the pie chart be? Circle the correct option.

    A 18°   **B** 163°   **C** 196°   **D** 198°   **E** 210°

Test 31

You have **10 minutes** to do this test. Work as quickly and accurately as you can.

1. Eva writes down some numbers on five cards, then places them in order of size.

   10.67   11.1   10.73   11.03   11.11

   Circle the number that is out of order.

   A   10.67   B   11.1   C   10.73   D   11.03   E   11.11

2. Mr Baker is preparing ingredients for a cookery class.
   He buys 1500 g of flour to be used by a class of 10 students.
   How many kg of flour would he need for a class of 40 students?

   Answer: _____ kg

3. Marie has $^7/_8$ of a box of cereal left. There are 24 servings in a full box.
   How many servings are left in the box?

   Answer: _____

4. In a class of 28 pupils, 7 wear glasses. Give the ratio of pupils who wear glasses to pupils who don't in its simplest form.

   Answer: _____ : _____

5. James takes straws of length 13.4 cm, 4.4 cm and 10.25 cm, and sticks them together, end-to-end. He uses the straws to try and reach his keys, which are 30 cm away. How far short of his keys will the end of the straws be?

Answer: _____ cm

6. A hand wash dispenser contains 300 ml of hand wash. It dispenses 5 ml of hand wash on each use. The dispenser is refilled when it is ³⁄₄ empty. After how many uses will this be? Circle the correct option.

   A 30   B 45   C 60   D 100   E 225

7. A carpenter makes tables and desks. From a 4 m × 4 m piece of wood, she cuts one circular table and four identical corner desks, as shown below.

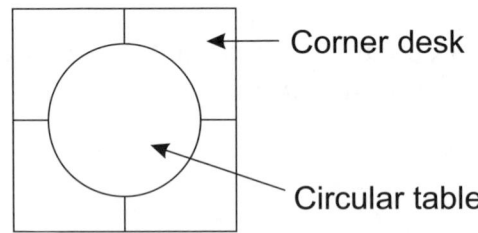

If the circular table has an area of 7 m², what is the area of one corner desk? Circle the correct option.

   A 1.75 m²   C 3.25 m²   E 3.75 m²
   B 2.25 m²   D 2.5 m²

8. A newspaper publishes the following graph on Saturday morning with the headline:

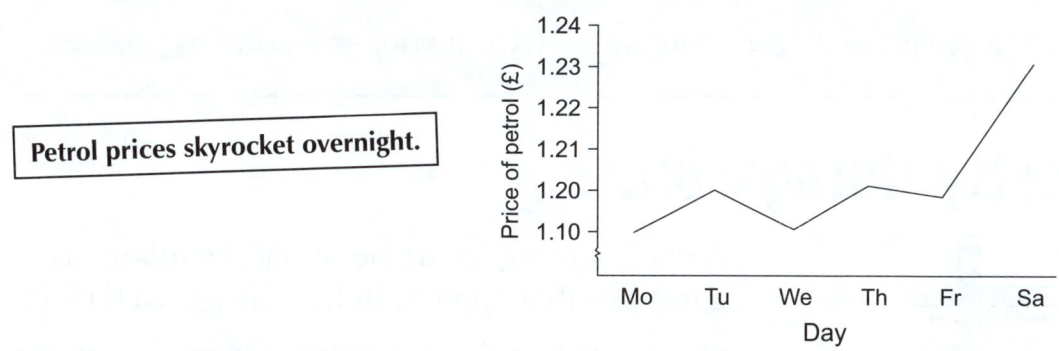

Why is the graph misleading? Circle the correct option.

    A   The graph doesn't write out the full date.
    B   The graph doesn't show the price of other fuels such as diesel.
    C   The price of petrol is constantly changing.
    D   The scale of the y-axis is uneven.
    E   The y-axis of the graph doesn't start at zero.

9. Sachin is given a kit containing 1573 toy construction blocks as a birthday present. He wants to split the blocks equally between himself and his 12 friends. How many blocks should he give to each of his friends?

Answer: _____

10. Gregory makes booklets for his jogging club. One sheet of paper folds to make 4 pages in the booklet, then a final sheet of paper which contains an advert is added. Which expression shows the total number of sheets of paper needed to make a booklet containing x pages? Circle the correct option.

    A $4x + 1$ **C** $x/4 + 1$ **E** $x + 1/4$
    B $x + 4$ **D** $4(x + 1)$

Puzzles 12

Now for a break from 10-minute tests. Try out your skills on this puzzle.

Ghostly Goings-on...

Anita is writing an article about the infamous ghost bus that appears in her village each night.

She wants to publish it in the school newspaper and is desperate to get a photo of the bus to go with her article, but she has no idea when it appears. She interviews some of her neighbours to gather information.

I lock up my barn at 19:10. The ghost bus appears 15 minutes later.

Sally Spooks

I take my dog for a walk at 19:40. The walk takes one hour and I always see the ghost bus when I'm halfway along the route.

Milly Midnight

I leave work at 5:32 pm and the ghost bus appears 35 minutes later.

Gary Ghoul

I hear the ghost bus two minutes before the end of my favourite TV show. It starts at 6:20 pm and lasts 25 minutes.

Phil Phantom

Use this information to work out what time each neighbour sees the ghost bus, then draw arrows on the timeline below that roughly point to each time. Label each arrow with the correct name and time so Anita knows where to go.

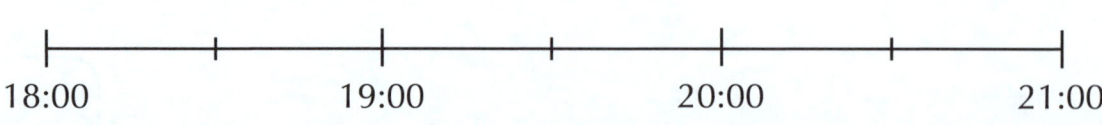

Answers

Test 1 — pages 2-4

1. 46 kg
You're rounding the 6, so look at the digit to the right. It's a 4, so you round down to 46 kg.

2. 98 641
To make the biggest number possible out of a set of digits, you just have to put them in descending order. So the biggest digit has the highest place value possible, all the way down to the smallest digit being the ones. In the five cards that Vivian has, the biggest number that can be made is 98 641.

3. D
She sells 2.5 books of 1000 tickets so that's 2.5 × 1000 = 2500 tickets. Each ticket is 10p, so she makes 2500 × 10p = 25 000p. To get from pence into pounds, you need to divide by 100, so 25 000p ÷ 100 = £250.

4. B
The total age of the dogs is:
1 + 3 + 4 + 5 + 8 + 8 + 13 = 42.
To find the mean age of the dogs, divide the total age by the number of dogs: 42 ÷ 7 = 6.

5. 29
Subtract the number of books with 300 or more pages from the total number of books:
100 − 19 − 22 − 30 = 29.

6. A
Convert all the times into minutes, and then add up the amount of time he spends on each chore:
45 + 50 + 25 = 120 minutes.
1 hour = 60 minutes, so 120 minutes = 2 hours.

7. 5
1.5 litres = 1500 ml. Subtract the amount used each day one at a time: 1500 − 100 = 1400 ml
1400 − 200 = 1200 ml
1200 − 300 = 900 ml
900 − 400 = 500 ml
500 − 500 = 0 ml
So after 5 days, Rob's bottle is empty.

8. 9.2 km
Convert the distance that is in miles into kilometres:
2 × 1.6 = 3.2 km. Then add all three distances together:
2.3 km + 3.7 km + 3.2 km = 9.2 km.

9. E
Angles in a circle add up to 360°, so to find out what angle would be used, find 20% of 360°:
10% of 360 = 360 ÷ 10 = 36°, so 20% = 36 × 2 = 72°.

10. 166°
To find the shaded angle, find the part of the angle that is in the triangle, and the part of the angle that is in the rectangle. The triangle is isosceles, so the two missing angles of the triangle are the same. They add up to 180 − 28 = 152°. So each one is 152 ÷ 2 = 76°.
The angles in a rectangle are all right angles, i.e. 90°. So the shaded angle is 76 + 90 = 166°.

Test 2 — pages 5-7

1. C
24 ÷ 3 = 8, 24 ÷ 4 = 6, 24 ÷ 12 = 2.

2. 100
The boxes are stacked in pairs, so for every box wide the sequence is, there are two boxes in total. So if the stack is 50 boxes wide, then there will be 2 × 50 = 100 boxes.

3. 7
```
   0 6 remainder 2
3 ) 2²0
```
If Charlie only buys 6 bags of hay, 2 hutches will be remaining — so he needs 7 bags.

4. £12
The area of the floor is 5 m × 6 m = 30 m². Each tin covers 10 m², so Joan will need 30 ÷ 10 = 3 tins of varnish. This will cost 3 × £4 = £12.

5. C
If the shape has four sides, then you know that the angles add up to 360°. So you already know that the answer to C is "Yes."

6. D
There are 5 cars, each of length 4 m, and 4 of the cars will have a 0.5 m gap in front of them (the car at the front of the line won't have a gap). So the total length of the cars is
(5 × 4) + (4 × 0.5) = 22 m.

7. C
The question asks for the mean number of cups from Monday to Friday, so firstly find the total number of cups from these days:
9 + 7 + 5 + 4 + 5 = 30. Then divide the total by the number of days: 30 ÷ 5 = 6.

8. 14 °C
75% of 8 °C is the same as $\frac{3}{4}$ of 8 °C. 8 ÷ 4 = 2, and 2 × 3 = 6 °C. So the temperature increased by 6 °C. 8 + 6 = 14 °C.

9. E
In the 12 m × 3 m × 2 m container, you could fit 6 boxes long, 3 boxes wide and 2 boxes high. So Jerry can fit 6 × 3 × 2 = 36 boxes into the shipping container.

10. C
The basic charge for staying at the campsite is £14. The cost per person is £4, so c campers will cost 4c. The cost per dog is £2, so d dogs will cost 2d. So the total cost is 14 + 4c + 2d.

Test 3 — pages 8-10

1. 38
Kylie's sequence is 10, 14, 18, 22, 26, 30, 34, 38...
Thea's sequence is 10, 17, 24, 31, 38...

2. 52.7 cm
```
    1 7 . 3
    2 0 . 1
 +  1 5 . 3
    5 2 . 7
        1
```

3. 6
There are 39 children in total. Subtract the number of girls to find the total number of boys: 39 − 23 = 16. Subtract the number of boys with a weekend birthday: 16 − 10 = 6.

4. 48
He uses 2 bags for every 3 cups, so split up the total number of cups he makes into threes. 72 ÷ 3 = 24
(you can find this by writing out the division or by partitioning 72 into 60 + 12). So Derek makes 24 lots of 3 cups. This means he uses 2 × 24 = 48 tea bags.

5. B
Each picture of a ticket represents 40 tickets sold. There are 4 whole pictures of tickets in the action row, which represent 4 × 40 = 160 tickets sold. There is also a quarter of one ticket picture, which represents $\frac{1}{4} \times 40 = 10$ tickets sold.
Adding these together gives: 160 + 10 = 170 tickets sold.

6. B
£1.50 = 150p. $\frac{1}{3}$ of 150 is 150 ÷ 3 = 50, so Alice saves 50p on each daily return bus fare. The travel card cost £15, which is 1500p. 1500 ÷ 50 = 30, so it will take 30 days for Alice's savings to equal the price of the travel card.

7. D
24th October is a Tuesday, so count on in sevens — 31st October is also a Tuesday, and in November the 7th and 14th are Tuesdays. Two days after this is Thursday 16th November.

8. 5
The carrots come in bags of 6, so the total number of carrots must be a multiple of 6. There are 10 horses who all get the same number, so the total number of carrots must also be a multiple of 10. The lowest common multiple of 6 and 10 is 30, so she buys 30 carrots. 30 ÷ 6 = 5, so she buys 5 bags.

9. A
The volume of the cube is 3 × 3 × 3 = 27 cm³.
The base of the pyramid has an area of 3 × 3 = 9 cm².
So the volume of the pyramid is:
$\frac{1}{3}$ × area of the base × height = $\frac{1}{3}$ × 9 × 3 = 9 cm³.
So the total volume of the shape is 27 + 9 = 36 cm³.

10. C
Half of a half is a quarter, so $\frac{1}{4}$ of his action figures are in their original packaging and limited edition. This means the total number of action figures in his collection can be divided exactly by 4. The only one of the options which can be divided exactly by 4 is 88 (88 ÷ 4 = 22).

Puzzles 1 — page 11

Which Planet Next?
You should have circled the planet that is 876 235 alien miles from Ali's current position.
Ali has 823 474 alien miles left to travel.

Test 4 — pages 12-14

1. 5:27 pm
Take 41 minutes off 6:08 pm to find the answer.
8 minutes before 6:08 pm is 6:00 pm. You need to take off another 33 minutes to make up a total of 41 minutes. 33 minutes before 6:00 pm is 5:27 pm.

2. E
When rounded to the nearest 100 ml, all of the other bottles round to 1000 ml. For 1055 ml, there is a 5 in the tens column, so the hundreds column rounds up to give 1100 ml instead of 1000 ml.

3. A
The number of lines of symmetry of a regular polygon is always the same as the number of sides (you can test this by drawing some different regular shapes). So the difference between them will be zero, no matter which regular polygon Mateo is thinking of.

4. 1200 minutes
Each week Betty does 30 × 5 = 150 minutes of yoga.
In 8 weeks she does 150 × 8 = 1200 minutes.

5. C
If all the votes were shown, then the percentages would add up to 100%. In the bar chart they only add up to 17 + 19 + 15 = 51%. So it looks like only 3 colours were voted for, but because not all of the votes are shown, there would have been other colours chosen.

6. 11 m
If the diameter of the whole dance floor is 30 m, then the radius is half of this: 30 ÷ 2 = 15 m. The radius of the blue circle is 4 m less than the radius of the whole dance floor, so it is 15 − 4 = 11 m.

7. 8 minutes
2 hours 40 minutes is 2 × 60 + 40 = 160 minutes.
Dividing this into 20 equal sessions gives 160 ÷ 20 = 8 minutes.

8. 7
Each apprentice builder gets £210 ÷ 7 = £30 a day. Qualified builders get paid three times as much, so £30 × 3 = £90 a day. The total for qualified builders is £630, so there are 630 ÷ 90 = 7 qualified builders. (You could also spot that the total wages of the qualified builders is three times greater than that of the apprentices: £210 × 3 = £630. As each qualified builder is paid three times more than each apprentice, there must be the same number of each.)

9. D
Arch is 39 − 22 = 17 km away from Copp. So a town that was the same distance away would have to be 39 + 22 = 61 km away from where Darren is. There is no town listed that far away, so it can't be any option with Arch in it. Barne is 39 − 32.5 = 6.5 km away from Copp. So a town that was the same distance away would have to be 39 + 6.5 = 45.5 km away from where Darren is. Erton is 45.5 km from Darren. So Barne and Erton are the same distance away from Copp.

10. 470
Put n = 10 into the formula:
$5(10)^2 - 3(10) = 5 \times 10^2 - 3 \times 10$
$= 5 \times 100 - 30 = 500 - 30 = 470$
Remember that 10^2 is just 10 × 10, which equals 100.

Test 5 — pages 15-17

1. A
5 g out of 50 g is fat. $\frac{5}{50}$ is equivalent to $\frac{10}{100}$ (multiply the numerator and the denominator by 2). $\frac{10}{100}$ is 10%.

2. 20 days
The number of days until they both go to the gym on the same day again must be a multiple of 4 and a multiple of 5. The lowest common multiple of 4 and 5 is 20. So they will both go to the gym on the same day again after 20 days.

Answers

3. C

A line going through the line AB at 90° looks like this:

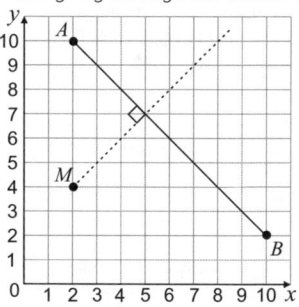

This line meets the line AB at the point (5, 7).

4. £6.01

Use the column method to add up how much his meal cost:

```
   8.95
   3.69
+  1.35
-------
  13.99
   1 1 1
```

Now subtract the cost of his meal from £20:
£20.00 − £13.99 = £6.01.

5. 9 litres

15 kg = 15 000 g. Each bowl weighs 500 g, so Angela can make 15 000 ÷ 500 = 30 bowls.
Each bowl holds 300 ml, so in total, all the bowls hold 30 × 300 = 9000 ml, which is equal to 9 litres.

6. C

It's easiest to treat the floor plan as 2 rectangles and add their areas together. The area of one rectangle is 6 × 3 = 18 m². The second rectangle has a height of 5 m and a width of 3 m (9 − 6 = 3). 5 × 3 = 15 m².
So the area of the room is: 15 + 18 = 33 m².

7. 1600 seconds

If $W = 20$, then:
$20W + 1200$
$= (20 \times 20) + 1200$
$= 400 + 1200 = 1600$ seconds.

8. D

6 bags divided between 15 dogs would give $^6/_{15}$ of a bag for each dog. This fraction can be simplified to $^2/_5$ if you divide the numerator and the denominator by 3.

9. 20

120° of the pie chart represents pumpkin, so 360° − 120° = 240° of the pie chart represents carrot. This as a fraction of the circle is $^{240}/_{360} = ^2/_3$.
So in the class of 30 children, $^2/_3$ said carrot.
$^2/_3$ of 30 is equal to 30 ÷ 3 × 2 = 20 children.

10. B

First work out how many beams he can lift in one go. The pulley system can support 65 kg, and each beams has a mass of 7 kg. 10 beams would have a total mass of 70 kg (which is too heavy), but 9 beams would have a total mass of 9 × 7 = 63 kg, so he can lift 9 beams each time. He has 100 beams, so divide this by the number of beams he can lift each time to find the number of times he will need to use the pulley system:

So raising the pulley 11 times will leave 1 beam left on the ground, and he will have to raise it a 12th time to lift the last beam.

Puzzles 2 — page 18

Time For a Brew
Hetty needs to put 2 bats, 4 spiders, 2 snakes and 2 lizards into the potion.

Herbal Medication
Hetty needs 18 g of hemlock, 12 g of crow feathers and 15 g of thistle.

Test 6 — pages 19-21

1. E

The person who was closest to the correct point is the one with the smallest value in the distance column. To find the smallest, first compare the units — Marshall, Ceri and Dan have the lowest units value (0). Now compare the tenths values for these three — Dan has the lowest tenths value (1), so Dan was the closest.

2. B

You can work this out using estimation. Round 112.3p to the nearest pound — this gives £1. So 30 litres will cost roughly £30. The only realistic option is £33.69.

3. Thursday

As you count on from Tuesday, you will return to Tuesday after every 7 days you count. Dividing 30 by 7 gives 4 remainder 2. After you've counted 4 lots of 7, you will be back on Tuesday. There are still 2 days left over, so Jim was born 2 days after Tuesday, which is Thursday.

4. 3

You can do this by just filling in the gaps in the 'Tails' column or the 'Blue' row. Filling in the 'Tails' column: the number of red tails is 19 − 5 = 14.
The total number of tails is 31 − 14 = 17.
So the number of blue tails is 17 − 14 = 3.

5. 15

The difference between terms in the sequence increases by 1 each time, so you can write down the sequence:

1, 3, 6, 10, 15...
 +2 +3 +4 +5

6. A

Subtract the new height from the original height to find how much it has grown: 12.8 − 8.0 = 4.8 cm.
1 cm = 10 mm, so 4.8 cm = 4.8 × 10 = 48 mm.
The flower grows 8 mm per month, so divide 48 by 8 to work out how many months Ashok has had the flower:
48 ÷ 8 = 6 months.

7. 50%
To add the fractions, you need to put them over the same denominator. Here, it's 10. $^1/_5 = {}^2/_{10}$, so a total of $^2/_{10} + {}^3/_{10} = {}^5/_{10} = {}^1/_2$ has been used. This means that there's still $^1/_2$ left, which is equivalent to 50%.

8. 36 m
The cuboid has 12 edges. You can see from the diagram that 8 of these have length 2.5 m, and 4 have length 4 m. So the total length of wire needed is
$8 \times 2.5 + 4 \times 4 = 20 + 16 = 36$ m.

9. A
There is a fixed charge of £15, so the first part of the expression will be '15 +'. Then there is a charge of £Y for every kg above 20 kg. For 24 kg, the charge will be $4 \times £Y$. So the expression is $15 + 4 \times Y$, which can be written as $15 + 4Y$.

10. C
The tie has been reduced by $20 - 16 = £4$, so it has been reduced by $^4/_{20}$. Multiplying the numerator and denominator by 5 gives $^{20}/_{100}$, so it has been reduced by 20%.

Test 7 — pages 22-24

1. C
Anna is rounding to the nearest 1000, so look at the hundreds. 8 is bigger than 5, so round up to 4 231 000. The 1 is in the thousands position.

2. B
From the front, you will see 5 squares side by side, with one square sticking out from the top of the second square from the left.

3. 15
If the ratio is 2:5, this means there should be 5 oranges for every 2 apples. 6 apples are used, which equals 3 lots of 2. So there should be $5 \times 3 = 15$ oranges.

4. 6.6 km
If 1 mile is 1.6 km, 2 miles = $2 \times 1.6 = 3.2$ km.
$3.2 + 3.4 = 6.6$ km in total.

5. C
Three out of four people gives the fraction $^3/_4$.
This is equivalent to 75% (multiplying the numerator and denominator by 25 gives $^{75}/_{100}$). So a greater proportion of people said they read The Morning Cable.

6. 420 ml
10% of 350 ml = 35 ml, so 20% of 350 ml is
$35 \times 2 = 70$ ml. Fluffy drinks 70 ml more than Mrs Tibbles, so Fluffy drinks: $350 + 70 = 420$ ml.

7. B
You know that the front row contains 10 seats, so that leaves $154 - 10 = 144$ seats remaining, spread over the 12 other rows. So divide the number of seats by the number of rows to find the number of seats per row:
$144 \div 12 = 12$.

8. 80 cm
Each triangle's perimeter is 26 cm and its base is 10 cm. This means that the two other sides of the triangle add up to $26 - 10 = 16$ cm. There are 5 triangles, so the total perimeter of the star is $5 \times 16 = 80$ cm.

9. C
He starts with £150, then gives away five lots of £P. So what he has left is '£150 minus five times £P', which is: $£150 - (5 \times £P)$. You don't need the brackets, so the final expression for what's left in pounds is: $150 - 5P$.

10. C
39.5 rounds up to 40 to the nearest mile.
To find the number of gallons of fuel required for a 440 mile journey, Mr Klein will divide 440 by 40:
$440 \div 40 = 11$ (use partitioning or long division to find this). So he estimates that he will need 11 gallons of fuel.
He rounded the number of miles per gallon up by 0.5, so for every gallon of fuel he uses, he will actually do 0.5 miles less than his estimate. Over 11 gallons of fuel, this will give a total difference of $11 \times 0.5 = 5.5$ gallons. So he will run out of fuel 5.5 miles short of his destination.

Test 8 — pages 25-27

1. 3824
To round to the nearest 10 and result in 3820, a number must be at least 3815 but less than 3825. Therefore, the largest whole number it can be is 3824.

2. 192
Looking at the table, you can see that the number of cows in the field increases by 11 every hour, meaning Mrs Finch is herding in 11 cows every hour. To find out how many cows will be in the field at 12:00, add 11 cows to the number at 11:00. $181 + 11 = 192$.

3. 2
Divide 100 by 7 to find the remainder:
$0\ 1\ 4\ \text{remainder 2}$
$7|1\,{}^10\,{}^30$
So there are 2 boxes left over.

4. 4
Reading from the bar chart, the most popular colour was red. Comparing the two bars, the blue bar is $^1/_3$ of the height of the red bar. $^1/_3$ of 12 is $12 \div 3 = 4$, so 4 pupils chose blue.

5. 33
Count up from 5 in steps of 7. The sequence is
5, 12, 19, 26, 33, 40, ... So John started counting back from 33.

6. D
2, 3, 5 and 7 are prime numbers.
4, 6, 8 and 9 are not prime numbers.

7. C
Add up the totals for 1-100 m, 101-200 m and 201-300 m to find the number of pupils that ran 300 m or less:
$4 + 6 + 12 = 22$.
There was a total of $4 + 6 + 12 + 8 = 30$ pupils, so the fraction you're looking for is $^{22}/_{30}$, which simplifies to $^{11}/_{15}$ (dividing the numerator and denominator by 2).

8. B
2 bottles of water cost $0.55 \times 2 = £1.10$.
So out of the £2.15 she spends, £1.10 is on water.
This leaves $£2.15 - £1.10 = £1.05$, which was spent on the 3 pieces of fruit (you can use the column method or partitioning for this subtraction).
Dividing this by 3 will give the price of one piece of fruit:
$0\ .\ 3\ 5$
$3|1\ .\ {}^10\ {}^15$
The cost of one piece of fruit was 35p, so it was a banana.

9. 113°
The second triangle on the track is a right-angled triangle, so the two angles given add up to 90 + 48 = 138°. Angles in a triangle add up to 180°, so the third angle is 180 − 138 = 42°. Angles on a straight line add up to 180°, so x + 25 + 42 = 180. 25 + 42 = 67, so x = 180 − 67 = 113°.

10. B
The y-axis has an x-coordinate of 0 and the corner of the square has an x-coordinate of −5, so you can see that the distance between the opposite corners of each square is 2 units: 2.5 squares × 2 units = 5 units.
The point marked A is 4 units right and 2 units up from point (0, 0). So the coordinates of point A are (4, 2).

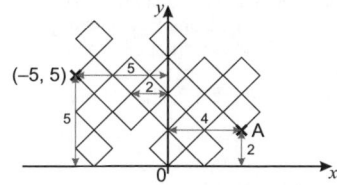

Puzzles 3 — page 28

Termsearch
a) obtuse   d) pictogram   g) estimate
b) hexagon   e) net   h) algebra
c) tally chart f) scalene

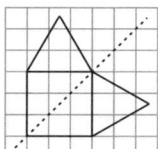

Test 9 — pages 29-31

1. 1.6 m
Subtract her distance from 40 m to find the difference.
38.4 breaks down into 38 + 0.4.
40 − 38 = 2, 2 − 0.4 = 1.6 m.

2. 5 hours
6 × 50 minutes = 300 minutes. 1 hour = 60 minutes, and 300 = 5 × 60, so 300 minutes = 5 hours.

3. 14
8 groups of 7 gives a total of 8 × 7 = 56 people. So divide 56 by 4 to find the number of groups of 4 they could have: 56 ÷ 4 = 14. Alternatively, you could spot the relationship between the numbers: 4 is half of 8, so the number you're looking for should be double 7.

4. C
Tamim wants a paddling pool 3.5 m wide, i.e. that has a diameter of 3.5 m. The radius of a circle is half its diameter, so Tamim needs the pool with the radius of 3.5 ÷ 2 = 1.75 m.

5. 22
25% of 100 = 25. The amount of people who chose ready salted = 100 − 25 + 53 = 100 − 78 = 22 people.

6. D
A, B, C and E are all equivalent to $^{10}/_9$. Dividing the numerator and denominator of $^{50}/_{45}$ by 5, $^{30}/_{27}$ by 3, $^{20}/_{18}$ by 2, and $^{40}/_{36}$ by 4 gives $^{10}/_9$ each time. $^{11}/_9$ is 11 ninths rather than 10 ninths, so it's not equivalent.

7. B
Look at the calculation and compare it to the calculation you're trying to find. You can see that both contain the number 215. If 6450 ÷ 30 = 215, then 215 × 30 = 6450.
60 is double 30, so the answer to 215 × 60 will be double the answer to 215 × 30.
That is 2 × 6450: 6000 × 2 = 12 000, and 450 × 2 = 900, so 2 × 6540 = 12 000 + 900 = 12 900.

8. E
The area of the floor including the island is 7 × 11 = 77 m². The island's area is 1.5 × 3 = 4.5 m². So the remaining floor space is 77 − 4.5 = 72.5 m².

9.
Add up the total number of apple pictures for Matt, Ami and Tej: $1^1/_4 + 2^1/_4 + 1^1/_2 = 3^1/_2 + 1^1/_2 = 5$ (the two lots of $^1/_4$ add up to make $^1/_2$). One apple picture represents 4 pieces of fruit, so 5 apple pictures represents 5 × 4 = 20 pieces of fruit. You're told that 23 pieces of fruit are eaten in total, so Nigel must eat 3 pieces. 3 is $^3/_4$ of 4, so the correct option is $^3/_4$ of an apple.

10. D
$^1/_3$ is the same as $^2/_6$, and 1 is the same as $^6/_6$.
So Jenny has $1 - ^1/_3 = ^6/_6 - ^2/_6 = ^4/_6$ of a bag left,
Iman has $1 - ^1/_6 = ^6/_6 - ^1/_6 = ^5/_6$ of a bag left and
Sara has $^1/_3 + ^1/_6 = ^2/_6 + ^1/_6 = ^3/_6$ of a bag.
So Iman has the most, then Jenny, then Sara.

Test 10 — pages 32-34

1. C
It has one diagonal line of symmetry:

2. D
She gets 1 point for each of her 12 correct answers, giving a total of 12 points. She then loses 1 point for each of her 15 incorrect answers, so she loses 15 points. This gives an overall score of 12 − 15 = −3 points.

3. 25
1 m = 100 cm, so 2.5 m = 2.5 × 100 = 250 cm. Dividing this into 10 cm ribbons will give 250 ÷ 10 = 25 pieces.

4. £14.50
They buy a total of 4 + 4 + 2 = 10 bottles, so the cost is £1.45 × 10 = £14.50.

5. D
If the marbles can't be divided into equal groups, then there must be a prime number of marbles. 41 is the only prime number listed.

6. 18 years
Kieran's age is a multiple of both 6 and 9, so it could be 18, 36, 54, 72, etc. Now subtract 2 from each of these until one of them gives a square number. 18 − 2 = 16, which is a square number, so he must be 18 years old.

7. B
In the pictogram, there are $5\frac{1}{2}$ wheels representing summer and $1\frac{1}{6}$ wheels representing winter.
Each wheel represents 6 bike rides, so Lauren went on $5\frac{1}{2} \times 6 = 33$ bike rides in summer and $1\frac{1}{6} \times 6 = 7$ bike rides in winter. Subtract to find the difference: 33 − 7 = 26.

8. 8 minutes
The mean time it took people to swim 500 m was 9 minutes, so the total of all the times is $5 \times 9 = 45$ minutes. The total time for Amelia, Samuel, Carolina and Arizona is 7 + 10 + 12 + 8 = 17 + 20 = 37 minutes. So Violet swam 500 m in 45 − 37 = 8 minutes.

9. C
Work backwards from the time she needs to arrive. She needs to be in Grizebell at 11:00, and it takes 20 minutes to get from Millon to Grizebell. 20 minutes before 11:00 is 10:40, so she needs to catch the last bus from Millon that leaves before 10:40. So the latest bus she could catch would be at 10:35 (remember the buses leave at 5 past and 35 past). It takes her 10 minutes to walk from home to the Millon bus stop, so she must leave no later than 10 minutes before 10:35, which is 10:25.

10. £1
First find the price of the jacket at Smart Togs: 10% of £55 = £5.50, so 20% = 2 × £5.50 = £11.
So the sale price is 55 − 11 = £44. Now find the price of the jacket at Top Garms: $\frac{1}{4}$ of 60 = 60 ÷ 4 = 15.
So the sale price is 60 − 15 = £45. So the price difference between the two shops is 45 − 44 = £1.

Puzzles 4 — page 35

The Scale Factor
Leaning Tower of Pisa = 56 m, Eiffel Tower = 27 m.
The artist's Leaning Tower of Pisa model would be 6 m taller if they had used a scale factor of 4.

Food Glorious Food
A is: 20-3-2011, B is: 16-5-2103,
C is: 6-12-1990, D is: 9-8-2083.
Tin B went out of date most recently.

Test 11 — pages 36-38

1. 20:45
Quarter to nine in the evening is the same as 8:45 pm. To convert to the 24-hour format, add 12 hours: 8:45 + 12:00 = 20:45.

2. Pentagon
The new shape is shown below:

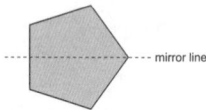

The shape has 5 sides, so it's a pentagon.

3. £240
Divide £400 by the total number of parts in the ratio to work out the value of 1 part. 4 + 6 = 10 parts, so 1 part = £400 ÷ 10 = £40. Brian earns 6 parts, so he earns £40 × 6 = £240.

4. D
A is incorrect because 23 can't be divided equally by 2.
B is incorrect because if Sheryl caught twice as many as Amanda, then their total would be 3 times as many as the number Amanda caught. But 23 can't be divided exactly by 3. Again, C is incorrect because 23 can't be divided exactly by 3.
E is incorrect because there is no combination of numbers that would match this description. For example, if Amanda caught 1 fish and Sheryl caught 10, then this would only give a total of 11. If Amanda caught 2 and Sheryl caught 20, then this would only give a total of 22. If Amanda caught 3 and Sheryl caught 30, then this would give a total of 33. Anything higher than that and the total will also be too large. D is correct because if Amanda caught 11 fish and Sheryl caught 12, then this would give a total of 23.

5. E
You need to divide $\frac{3}{4}$ by 2. To divide a fraction by a whole number, multiply the denominator by the whole number. So $\frac{3}{4} \div 2 = \frac{3}{8}$

6. 11:30 am
When the graph is moving upwards, Alejandro's distance from home is increasing, so he is moving away from home. When the graph is moving downwards, his distance from home is decreasing, so he is getting closer to home. So the point that he turns around is the point that the graph changes direction from moving upwards to moving downwards. This is when the value on the time axis is 30 minutes. He set off at 11:00 am, so he changed direction at 11:00 + 30 minutes = 11:30 am

7. A
At the end of the first month, Alyssa will have £410 + £200 = £610. Adding £200 each month, she will have £810 after 2 months, £1010 after 3 months, £1210 after 4 months and £1410 after 5 months. So after 5 months, she will have enough to afford the £1350 car.

8. $\frac{5}{12}$
Put the fractions over a common denominator. Here, it is 12. $\frac{1}{4} = \frac{3}{12}$ and $\frac{1}{3} = \frac{4}{12}$. This means that $\frac{3}{12} + \frac{4}{12} = \frac{7}{12}$ of the calls are from his mum or dad.
To work out what fraction are from his girlfriend, subtract $\frac{7}{12}$ from 1. $1 = \frac{12}{12}$, so $\frac{12}{12} - \frac{7}{12} = \frac{5}{12}$.

9. B
The volume of the storage room is $4 \times 6 \times 8 = 192$ m^3.
The volume of the cube is $2 \times 2 \times 2 = 8$ m^3.
So the remaining volume is 192 − 8 = 184 m^3.

10. D
1 lasagne feeds 4 people, so 3 lasagnes will feed $4 \times 3 = 12$ people. There are 14 people altogether, so an extra $\frac{1}{2}$ a lasagne is needed to feed the remaining 2 people. 3 lasagnes need 500 g × 3 = 1500 g of mince, and $\frac{1}{2}$ a lasagne needs 500 g ÷ 2 = 250 g of mince.
So the total amount of mince needed is:
1500 g + 250 g = 1750 g.

Test 12 — pages 39-41

1. 17.5 seconds
You're rounding the 4. The number to the right of this is 6, so you round up to 17.5 seconds.

2. 23
Look at the non-fiction column. She has 51 non-fiction books in total, of which 28 are hardback. So she has 51 − 28 = 23 non-fiction paperbacks. (You could also work this out using the paperback row, calculating 62 − 39.)

3. £71.91
Using rounding, £7.99 to the nearest whole pound is £8. Multiply £8 by the number of puzzles: £8 × 9 = £72. You need to subtract the 9 pennies you added when you rounded up the original £7.99 price (9 lots of 1 pence). Subtract 9p from £72 −9p = £71.91.

4. E
To convert a percentage into a fraction, write the percentage as the numerator and 100 as the denominator: $^{20}/_{100}$. You can then simplify the fraction: $^{20}/_{100}$ can be rewritten as $^{1}/_{5}$, as both 20 and 100 are divisible by 5.

5. D
In the 10 cm × 8 cm × 2 cm box, you could fit 1 bar long, 2 bars wide and 4 bars high. So Philippa would be able to fit 1 × 2 × 4 = 8 chocolate bars into the box.

6. C
At Richdale's stadium, $^{3}/_{4}$ of 10 000 seats are taken:
$^{3}/_{4}$ of 10 000 = 10 000 ÷ 4 × 3 = 7500.
At Tottington's stadium, $^{1}/_{2}$ of 25 000 seats are taken:
$^{1}/_{2}$ of 25 000 = 25 000 ÷ 2 = 12 500.
So the headline is false — Tottington had more fans attending. Subtract to find the difference: 12 500 − 7500 = 5000, so Tottington had 5000 more fans attending.

7. C
If his speech starts at 11:50 am and is 35 minutes long then it ends at 12:25 pm. So count on from then until 4:20 pm to find the difference — four hours after 12:25 pm is 4:25 pm. Taking away 5 minutes from this gives 4:20 pm. So the difference is 3 hours 55 minutes.

8. B
The three given corners are shown as dots, so the jewel will be hidden at the point marked with a cross.
This has coordinates (5, 2).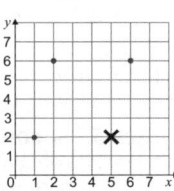

9. £49.45
Calculate how much profit he makes on each hot dog by subtracting 85p from £2. 2 − 0.85 = £1.15. To find how much money he makes in total, multiply £1.15 by 43 (you can use partitioning): £1 × 43 = £43, £0.10 × 43 = £4.30, £0.05 × 43 = £2.15. £43 + £4.30 + £2.15 = £49.45.

10. C
Add up the total number of all the birds:
50 + 30 + 100 + 20 = 200. 20 of the 200 birds are vultures, which is the same as 10%. Angles in a circle always add up to 360°, so the angle of the pie chart for vultures will be 10% of 360° = 360 ÷ 10 = 36°.

Test 13 — pages 42-44

1. 25.16 °C
The larger divisions go up by one decimal place each time. The line on the thermometer reaches the sixth smaller division between 25.1 and 25.2, so it is 25.16 °C.

2. B
Firstly, work out the factors of 33: 1, 3, 11 and 33. The amount has to have two digits, which rules out 1 and 3. It also needs to be a prime number, meaning 33 is ruled out (as it is divisible by 3 and 11), so the answer must be 11.

3. 28
Those who don't have to resit are the ones that scored 7 or more. So adding together the bars for 7-10 gives:
7 + 12 + 6 + 3 = 28 pupils.

4. D
120 cm = 1.2 m. Three lengths of 120 cm is equal to 3 × 1.2 = 3.6 m. Subtract this from the starting length: 40 − 3.6 = 36.4 m.

5. 40%
Find out how many games Jerry lost: 40 − 24 = 16. This can be written as $^{16}/_{40}$, which simplifies to $^{2}/_{5}$ (divide the numerator and denominator by 8). $^{2}/_{5}$ is equivalent to 40%.

6. C
Round the number of cakes up to 150 000 so it is easier to divide. Then round the number of weeks in the year down to 50. 150 000 ÷ 50 = 3000, so the average number of cakes made per week will be around 3000, but much closer to 3000 than to 1500, 5000 etc.

7. D
The mean mark was 8, and there were 5 pupils altogether, so the total of all the marks must have been 8 × 5 = 40. The total of the 4 marks you know is 9 + 7 + 8 + 6 = 30. So Eleanor's mark was 40 − 30 = 10.

8. A
The new shape will have 6 faces, each of area 6 cm². So the area of paper needed will be 6 × 6 = 36 cm².

9. 5955 ml
Terry is away for 4.5 hours. During this time, the bucket will have leaked 4.5 × 10 ml = 45 ml of water.
6 litres = 6000 ml, so the amount left in the bucket will be 6000 − 45 = 5955 ml (you can do this subtraction using partitioning or the column method).

10. 7 m
The length of lounge is $^{3}/_{4}$ the length of the kitchen:
$^{3}/_{4}$ of 28 m = 28 ÷ 4 × 3 = 21 m. To find the diameter of the pond, work out 28 − 21 = 7 m.

Puzzles 5 — page 45
Robert's Reflections
Your completed grid should look like this:

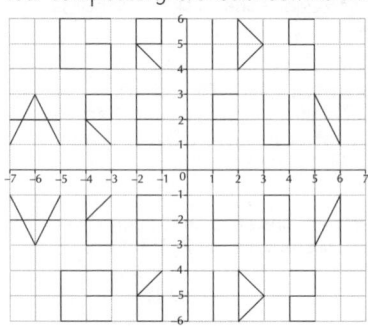

Test 14 — pages 46-48
1.   189 000 miles
You are rounding to the nearest thousand, so look at the figure in the hundreds column. It's a 4, so round down to 189 000 miles.

2.   B
Divide the amount he has by the amount he needs to make one cake:

```
         0 1 0 remainder 25
    30 ) 3¹2²5
```
So he can make 10 cakes with 25 g of chocolate chips left over.

3.   £2.46
Use partitioning to subtract how much she left with from how much she had at first: £3.20 − £0.70 = £2.50.
£2.50 − £0.04 = £2.46.

4.   14 200 g
14 kg = 14 000 g. Add this to the weight of the sack:
14 000 + 200 = 14 200 g.

5.   D
A cannot be true because all the interior angles in a regular polygon are equal.
B cannot be true because 360° ÷ 6 = 60°, but all of the interior angles in a hexagon are more than 90°.
C can't be true because only opposite sides in a regular hexagon are parallel.
E cannot be true because the angle is bigger than 90°.
D must be true because all sides in a regular polygon are the same length.

6.   £20.97
With the special offer, Eddie only needs to pay for 3 bags (he will get the other 3 bags for free). So it will cost 3 × £6.99.
Round £6.99 up to £7, then 3 × £7 = £21. Now subtract the 3 lots of 1p that you added when rounding to get the exact answer: £21 − 3p = £20.97.

7.   £29 500
Replace p with 300 in the formula. 15(300) + 25 000
= 15 × 300 + 25 000 = 4500 + 25 000 = £29 500
(you can use the partitioning or column method here).

8. $1/2$
To find $3/4$ of $2/3$, multiply the numerators together and multiply the denominators together: 3 × 2 = 6, and 4 × 3 = 12, so Darius has given $6/12$ of the chocolate bar to his friends. This can be simplified to give $1/2$.

9.   B
Follow the directions given for each possible answer. By doing this, you can see that B gave the right directions from P to S:

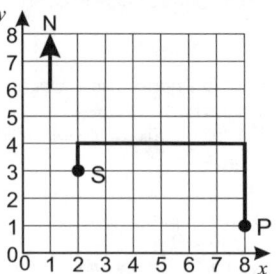

10.   E
Angles in a circle always add up to 360°, so subtract the angles of the other three sandwiches from 360° to find the angle of the egg sector:
360 − 160 − 100 − 64 = 36°. This is the same as saying $36/360$ said egg was their favourite. To work out how many out of 60 people said egg, divide the numerator and denominator by 6 to give $6/60$.

Test 15 — pages 49-51
1.   4
Martin's shape has four lines of symmetry: one horizontal, one vertical and two diagonal:

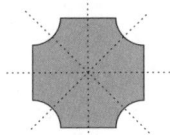

2.   E
15 is the only option that isn't a square number, so E must be correct (9 = 3^2, 25 = 5^2, 16 = 4^2, 4 = 2^2).

3.   27
The colours that begin with 'B' are blue, brown and black. Adding together the values in the bar chart for these colours gives: 2 + 11 + 14 = 27 houses.

4.   B
There are 60 minutes in one hour, so in each minute he flies 120 ÷ 60 = 2 km, which is equal to 2000 m.

5.   5 minutes 55 seconds
Subtracting 23 seconds off Indira's time gives 6 minutes. You need to subtract 5 more seconds to find Zoe's time, which is 5 minutes 55 seconds.

6.   £40
Add up the cost of each item to find the total amount he spent:
```
    8.00
   12.50
    3.50
    5.00
 +  7.50
   36.50
    2 1
```
Now add on the amount of change he received to find the amount he handed over: £36.50 + £3.50 = £40 (you can use the column method or partition £3.50 into £3 + 50p to find this).

7.   12
Pattern 1 has 3 marbles, pattern 2 has 5 marbles, and pattern 3 has 7 marbles, so you're adding two marbles each time. Count up, adding 2 each time, until you get to 25 marbles. This will be in pattern 12. (You could also notice that if you multiply the pattern number by 2 and add 1 then you get the number of marbles.)

8.   E
As you go up the vertical axis, the numbers go down from 0 to −10. This is misleading, because it looks like Friday and Saturday had the highest average temperature, but they actually had the lowest.

9.   £3
$3/8$ of £120 = 120 ÷ 8 × 3 = £45 and
$3/5$ of £120 = 120 ÷ 5 × 3 = £72. So Antonia's total spend on food and furniture is £45 + £72 = £117. This means she has £120 − £117 = £3 remaining.

10.   C
20 g of food is eaten each day, so the amount over n days will be $20n$. The amount remaining after n days will be the amount he started with, minus $20n$: $560 − 20n$.

Puzzles 6 — page 52

A Bond of Trust
The ring's rightful owner is Georgia.

Test 16 — pages 53-55

1.   pm
The hour number is more than 12, so it is pm.

2.   D
Sam is shortest, as she has the smallest tenths value (4). Len, Ash and Rod all have the same tenths value (5), so look at the hundredths value. Len is second shortest overall, as his hundredths value is 2, then Ash, who has a hundredths value of 6, and finally Rod is the tallest, with a hundredths value of 8.

3.   179
```
    4 7
    5 6
    5 2
+   2 4
  -----
  1 7 9
    1 1
```

4.   £50
Work out $1/3$ of the original price:
$1/3$ of £75 = 75 ÷ 3 = £25.
Now subtract this from the original price:
£75 − £25 = £50.

5.   36
List the square numbers less than 100:
1, 4, 9, 16, 25, 36, 49, 81.
Only three of those are a multiple of 9:
9 = 9 × 1, 36 = 9 × 4, 81 = 9 × 9.
Only one of those has 4 as a factor: 36.

6.   B
Each price has been rounded down by 5p.
There are 1 + 2 + 3 = 6 kg of fruit altogether.
So the incomplete calculation is 6 × 5p = 30p less than the exact amount, and so you need to add 30p.

7.   8 miles
Add up the distances that each train travels in a day:
Train A: 240 + 315 = 555 miles
Train B: 264 + 299 = 563 miles
(You can find these using the partitioning or the column method.) Now subtract the distance that train A travels from the distance train B travels:
563 − 555 = 8 miles.

8.   225°
Spinning 135° clockwise is the same as spinning 360 − 135 = 225° anticlockwise.

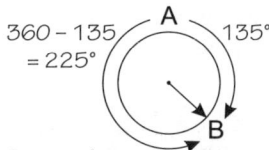

9.   A
The shape has been reflected vertically, so the x-coordinate is still the same (4). The y-coordinate of point X is 8, and the y-coordinate of the mirror line is 5. So, point X is 8 − 5 = 3 squares away from the mirror line.
The reflected point X will also be 3 squares away from the mirror line. So the y-coordinate will be 5 − 3 = 2.
The coordinates of the reflected point X are (4, 2).

10.   A
The number of blue bricks increases by 3 each time, so your formula should start with '$3n$'. The number of blue bricks in each pattern is 1 less than what you get if you multiply n by 3, so it must be $3n − 1$. (Instead, you could just try out each of the formulas in A-E and see which one works for all the patterns.)

Test 17 — pages 56-58

1.   E
The number 4 is in the 'hundred thousands' column, so it represents 400 000 (four hundred thousand).

2.   E
If a shape has perpendicular sides then it has a right angle. A square and a rectangle both have four right angles. An irregular pentagon could have one or more right angles. A triangle can also have a right angle (in a right-angled triangle). But a rhombus can never have a right angle.

3.   54
To find out how many visitors the site got in previous months you need to divide by 10. So in month three it got 54 000 ÷ 10 = 5400 visitors. In month two it got 5400 ÷ 10 = 540 visitors, and in month one it got 540 ÷ 10 = 54 visitors.

4.   120
To find the mean of 20 numbers, you divide the total of the numbers by 20. So to get from the mean to the total, multiply by 20. 6 × 20 = 120, so the total number of cousins is 120.

5.   C
On the vertical scale, the Police Officers' car is twice as tall as the Doctors' car, but it is also twice as wide. This makes it look like the Police Officers drive much more than double the number of miles than the Doctors.

6.   C
In total, there are 5 whole disc pictures and 2 half-disc pictures. The 2 halves make 1 more whole picture, so there are 6 in total. 3 of these are for reggae, so half of the teachers said that reggae was their favourite.
$3/6 = 1/2 = 50\%$.

7. £76
Divide £836 by 11 using long division.

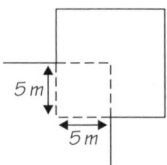

She spends £76 on each grandchild.

8. B
To work out what $^4/_5$ of $^1/_4$ is, you need to multiply the two fractions: $^1/_4 \times {^4/_5} = {^4/_{20}}$. You can then divide both the numerator and denominator by 4 to get $^1/_5$.

9. D
It would've taken one robot three times as long to clear the field — i.e. 3 hours. Two robots could've done it in half the time that one robot could, so it would've taken them $3 \div 2 = 1.5$ hours, or 1 hour and 30 minutes.

10. 240 m
The perimeter of the outer wall of the castle was originally $50 + 30 + 50 + 30 = 160$ m. The perimeter of one turret is $4 \times 10 = 40$ m. So the total perimeter of the outer wall and four turrets is: $160 + 4 \times 40 = 160 + 160 = 320$ m. But this includes four 5 m × 5 m squares that should not be included in the outer perimeter:

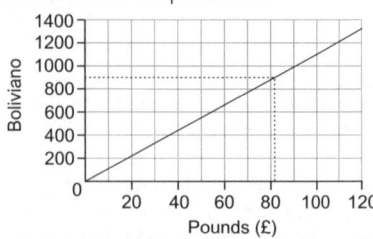

The perimeter of each of these small squares is $4 \times 5 = 20$ m. There are four of them, so take them away from the total: $320 - (4 \times 20) = 320 - 80 = 240$ m.

Test 18 — pages 59-61

1. C
$2 \times 10 = 20$, $5 \times 4 = 20$.

2. £255 000
Harry's car cost £255 × 100 = £25 500.
Bobby's car cost £25 500 × 10 = £255 000.

3. A
Draw a line from 900 bolivianos to the conversion line, then down to the pound axis:

It's around £80, so £82 (A) is the only suitable option.

4. 32%
First, work out the total number of pupils in the class: $8 + 17 = 25$. The fraction that said "no" was $^8/_{25}$. Multiply the denominator and numerator by four to get $^{32}/_{100}$. So the percentage is 32%.

5. 45 g
Divide the total mass by 3 to find the mass of one bag: From the 3 times tables, you know that $3 \times 9 = 27$, so $3 \times 90 = 270$. This means one bag has a 90 g mass. She eats half of this, which is $90 \div 2 = 45$ g.

6. 11th July
There are 30 days in June, so 30th June is $30 - 16 = 14$ days after Andrew's birthday. You need to count on another $25 - 14 = 11$ days into July, so Catherine's birthday is 11th July.

7. A
The towers at the back of the castle are made from cubes. The walls are all cuboids. The roof at the front of the castle is a triangular prism. The roofs of the towers are square-based pyramids. The only shape not used is a tetrahedron.

8. 6
The sequence starts with 6. Subtracting 3 gives $6 - 3 = 3$. Doubling this gives $3 \times 2 = 6$. So each time you perform the rule you get the same result, so every term in the sequence will be 6.

9. £33.30
6 hardback books cost $6 \times £4.50 = £27$ (you can use partitioning here). 4 paperback books cost $4 \times £2.50 = £10$. So Karina's order is $£27 + £10 = £37$. This is over £20, so she gets a 10% discount. 10% of £37 is £3.70, so her order comes to a total of $£37 - £3.70 = £33.30$.

10. 12 hours 30 minutes
For every 60 seconds Ryan travels, John has to travel for 1 hour 15 mins. There are 10 lots of 60 seconds in 10 mins. So multiply 1 hour 15 mins by 10:
1 hour × 10 = 10 hours. 15 mins × 10 = 150 mins, which is the same as 2 hours 30 mins (remember that 2 hours is 120 mins). Adding these together gives:
10 hours + 2 hours 30 mins = 12 hours 30 minutes.

Puzzles 7 — page 62

Sale Shopping
The new prices are: t-shirt = £17, book = £7.50, scooter = £24, bag = £9, necklace = £7, cup and saucer = £6.50.
If Anika spent exactly £40, she must have bought the scooter, the bag and the necklace.
Anika has saved £60 in the sale.

Test 19 — pages 63-65

1. 27
Reading the values for the height of each bar on the chart and adding them together gives:
$5 + 7 + 9 + 2 + 4 = 27$.

2. 11.2 kg
```
   4 . 1
   3 . 7
   1 . 2
+  2 . 2
-------
 1 1 . 2
   1 1
```

3. B
The difference between 10 and 1 is 9, and the difference between 1 and −8 is also 9. So the rule for the sequence is 'subtract 9 from the previous number'. The first number in the sequence is 28, so the missing second number will be $28 - 9 = 19$.

4. 4 mm
6 cm = 60 mm. If all the dominoes are the same thickness, then each one is 60 ÷ 15 = 4 mm thick.

5. E
The blue shape has one horizontal line of symmetry. By adding A or C, the line of symmetry remains exactly the same. By adding B or D, the line of symmetry changes to being diagonal, for example:

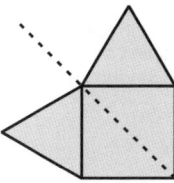

So the number of lines of symmetry is still one. By adding shape E, there is now an extra line of symmetry:

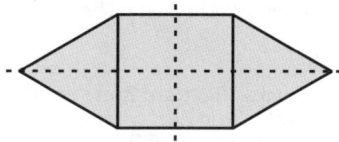

6. D
2.5 litres = 2500 ml.
8 × 300 = 2400, and 9 × 300 = 2700.
So there's only enough to completely fill 8 flasks.

7. 14
Work out how many bracelets he can make with the beads he has:

```
    0 6 2 remainder 2
4 ) 2 2 5 1 0
```

He can only make 62 bracelets, so 76 − 62 = 14 children will be left without a bracelet.

8. 5
The factors of 15 are 1, 3, 5 and 15. The square numbers under 15 are 1, 4 and 9. Only 1 and 4 add together to give a factor of 15: 1 + 4 = 5. So the chicken lays 5 eggs.

9. D
She moves nine units to the right (east), four units down (south), and then six units to the left (west), ending up at point D:

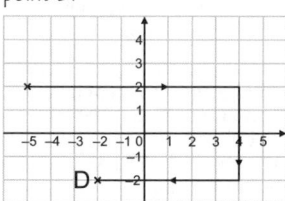

10. B
The number of matchsticks increases by 4 each time, so your formula should start with '4n'. The number of matchsticks in each pattern is 3 less than what you get if you multiply n by 4, so it must be 4n − 3. (Instead, you could just try out each of the formulas in A-E and see which one works for all the patterns.)

Test 20 — pages 66-68

1. 18 500 miles
You are rounding to the nearest hundred, so look at the figure in the 'tens' column. It's an 8, so you need to round up to 18 500 miles.

2. C
She will receive 50p for swimming one length, and so will receive £1 for every 2 lengths. So to reach £50, she will have to swim 50 × 2 = 100 lengths. (Alternatively, you could spot that £50 is 100 times bigger than 50p, so she'll have to swim 100 lengths.)

3. £9.50
Jack buys 4 ice creams: 4 × £1.25 = £5.00. He also buys 4 cold drinks: 4 × £0.70 = £2.80. He also buys 2 ice lollies: 2 × £0.85 = £1.70. So in total Jack spent £5.00 + £2.80 + £1.70 = £9.50.

4. E
A is incorrect because 6 is an even multiple of 3. B is incorrect because this is the description of a prime number, and square numbers aren't prime. C is incorrect because 2 is an even prime number. D is incorrect because 10, 20, 30 etc... are multiples of 5 that don't end in 5. E is correct because adding two odd numbers together gives an even number — so adding another odd number to this gives an odd number.

5. 5
You can see from the chart that the January row has an extra $1/4$ of a tyre picture compared to the February row. One tyre picture represents 20 people, and $1/4$ of 20 = 20 ÷ 4 = 5. So 5 more people passed their test in January than in February.

6. D
Aslan's friends share $4/4 - 1/4 = 3/4$ of the pie between them. So each friend has $3/4 ÷ 2$ of the pie to eat. When dividing a fraction by a whole number, you multiply the denominator by the whole number: 4 × 2 = 8, so his friends each had $3/8$ of the pie to eat.

7. C
Adding together the parallel sides gives 11 + 7 = 18 m. Halving this gives 18 ÷ 2 = 9 m. Multiplying this by the height gives 9 × 5 = 45 m².

8. B
When net B is folded up, the shaded faces in the diagram below would be in the same place:

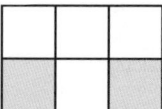

So it doesn't form an open-topped box.

9. C
Add up the totals for each film type to find which was the most popular:
Sci-Fi: 7 + 1 + 11 = 19
Western: 8 + 2 + 12 = 22
Rom-Com: 2 + 14 + 1 = 17
The highest overall total is Western, so A is true.
In the Maths Club row, the highest number is in the Rom-Com column, so B is true.
Add up the numbers in the Swimming Club row to find the number of members: 7 + 8 + 2 = 17, so C is false.
In the Art Club row, add up the values from the Sci-Fi and Western columns: 11 + 12 = 23, so D is true.
Add up the totals for the Art and Maths Club rows:
Art Club: 11 + 12 + 1 = 24
Maths Club: 1 + 2 + 14 = 17
24 − 17 = 7, so E is true.

10.   5.1 kg
The scales show that one giant cupcake weighs 170 g.
So 30 giant cupcakes weigh 170 × 30 = 5100 g,
which is equal to 5.1 kg.

Puzzles 8 — page 69
Marble Muddle
Penny has lost 12 red marbles, 18 blue marbles,
10 yellow marbles and 20 green marbles.

Flying Fish
Hector has an estimated fin area of 64 cm².
Horace has an estimated fin area of 63 cm².
So Hector has the largest estimated fin area.

Test 21 — pages 70-72
1.   30 °C
Find the difference between the two temperatures:
21 °C − − 9 °C = 21 + 9 = 30 °C.

2.   £600
25% of £800 = £800 ÷ 4 = £200.
Subtract 25% from the original price to find the sale price:
£800 − £200 = £600.

3.   24
The number of counters are doubling each time. So on her
fourth turn, she would place twice as many counters as on her
third turn: 12 × 2 = 24.

4.   C
C is the only shape with one line of symmetry:

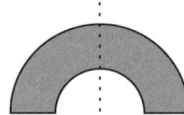

A has no lines of symmetry, and B, D and E have more than one.

5.   170 cm
1.2 m = 120 cm. If Gita grew 10 cm every year for five years,
then she grew 5 × 10 = 50 cm in total. So on her fifteenth
birthday, Gita would be 120 + 50 = 170 cm tall.

6.   A
You can make this calculation easier: 150 ÷ 20 is the
same as 15 ÷ 2, because both numbers in the calculation
are divided by 10. So do this division instead.
```
    0 7 remainder 1
  2 ) 1 ¹5
```
7 buckets won't be enough, so he will need 8 buckets.

7.   £129
The total amount she gets from selling the cupcakes
and biscuits is:
40 × £1.50 + 100 × £0.80 = £60 + £80 = £140
(you can partition £1.50 into £1.00 + £0.50 to help with this
bit). Now subtract the amount she spent on ingredients to find
her profit: £140 − £11 = £129.

8.   120 m³
The small cuboid has volume 2 × 3 × 4 = 24 m³.
The bigger cuboid has length 4 + 2 = 6 m, and has
width 3 + 1 = 4 m. Its height is 4 m, so its volume
is 6 × 4 × 4 = 96 m³. So the total volume is
24 + 96 = 120 m³.

9.   D
You can see from the graph that after her third go, she will be
at the point (6, 6). On her fourth go, she will move 4 spaces up
and 4 spaces to the right, so both the x-coordinate and the
y-coordinate will increase by 4, taking her to the point (10, 10).
On her fifth go, she will move 5 spaces up and 5 spaces to
the right, so both the x-coordinate and the y-coordinate will
increase by 5, taking her to the point (15, 15).

10.   E
Every month Sam saves £50, so after x months he will have
saved x lots of £50, which gives $50x$. Adding this to the
amount he has to start with (£350) gives the amount he has
after x months: $350 + 50x$.

Test 22 — pages 73-75
1.   C
The youngest tree will have been planted most recently and
so will have been planted in the year with the highest number.
1991 is the highest of the years and so the Ash is the
youngest tree.

2.   9
Split the calculation down into chunks. There are 2 lots of 50p
in £1, so there are 4 × 2 = 8 lots of 50p in £4.
Then there's one extra 50p to take it up to £4.50,
which gives 9 lots of 50p altogether.

3.   9
Each picture represents 6 muffins. Wednesday has
1 ½ more pictures than Friday. ½ a picture represents
6 ÷ 2 = 3 muffins, so 6 + 3 = 9 more muffins were sold on
Wednesday than on Friday.

4.   155 cm
There are two sides of length 35 cm and two sides
of length 42.5 cm. So the total length will be:
35 + 35 + 42.5 + 42.5 = 155 cm.

5.   D
Divide 140 by 12 using long division.
```
      0 1 1 remainder 8
  12 ) 1 4 0
       −1 2 ↓
          2 0
         −1 2
            8
```
There is a remainder of 8, so 11 crates wouldn't be enough —
there would be 8 tins left over, so 12 crates are needed.

6.   23
It's a prime number between 20 and 50, and the sum of its
digits equals a prime number less than 10, so it could be
23, 41 or 43, since 2 + 3 = 5, 4 + 1 = 5, and
4 + 3 = 7. Add 2 to each of these to see which makes
a square number: 41 + 2 = 43, 43 + 2 = 45, and
23 + 2 = 25. 25 is equal to 5², so Ted has 23 pigs.

7.   A
To add ¼ to ³⁄₈, you need to put them over
the same denominator, which is 8 here.
¼ = ²⁄₈, so ¼ + ³⁄₈ = ²⁄₈ + ³⁄₈ = ⁵⁄₈.
The full pie is ⁸⁄₈ ('eight lots of one eighth'),
so what's left over is: ⁸⁄₈ − ⁵⁄₈ = ³⁄₈

8. D
In a bar chart, each bar should represent an option, not its number. In this bar chart, each bar represents a number, which is misleading. The biggest bar goes to white, but only 1 person said white whereas 7 people said red.

9. 32
There are 44 biscuits in total, and 20 more ginger than chocolate. If you take away the 20 extra ginger ones, then you will have 24 biscuits in total — half will be ginger and half will be chocolate. So there will be 12 ginger and 12 chocolate. Now adding back on the extra 20 ginger ones, there are 32 ginger biscuits and 12 chocolate biscuits.

10. E
The area of the triangle is $1/2 \times$ base $\times$ height = $1/2 \times 7 \times 6 = 1/2 \times 42 = 21$ cm².
The area of the rectangle is $60 \times 7 = 420$ cm².
So the total area of one fence post is $420 + 21 = 441$ cm², and the area of the whole fence is $441 \times 100 = 44\ 100$ cm².

Test 23 — pages 76-78

1. 8 m
There are 10 divisions between 0 m and 20 m, so each one is worth 20 m $\div 10 = 2$ m.
The arrow is pointing 4 divisions past 0 m, so it's at $0 + (2 \times 4) = 8$ m.

2. Lorry and bus
When presenting data in a pie chart, the proportion of something is shown through the size of each sector. Because the lorry and bus sectors are the same size, there must have been the same number of lorries and buses.

3. 1.2 m
Twelve times longer than 10 cm is $10 \times 12 = 120$ cm $= 1.2$ m.

4. A
The left-hand circle has a right-angled triangle and a rectangle inside. Both of these shapes have at least one right angle, so A could be used. The right-angled triangle doesn't have any parallel lines or equal sides, so B and C can't be correct. There is a triangle in the right-hand circle, so D can't be correct. Neither of the shapes in the left-hand circle have obtuse angles, so E can't be correct.

5. C
Add up the amounts to find the total that he spent.
$2.20 + 1.80 + 1.65 + 1.70 = £7.35$ (use the partition method or column method to find this). However much he paid with was 65p more than this, so add on the 65p to find out how much: $£7.35 + 65p = £8.00$.

6. D
To find the answer, take 27 minutes off 14:12.
12 minutes before 14:12 is 14:00. You need to take off another 15 minutes to make up a total of 27 minutes.
15 minutes before 14:00 is 13:45.

7. Monday
Reading off the graph, Andrei reaches 250 km between numbers 14 and 15:

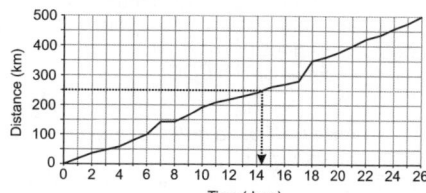

The day between numbers 0 and 1 is Monday. So counting on in sevens, the day between numbers 7 and 8 is a Monday, and so is the day between numbers 14 and 15. This is the time where Andrei reached 250 km, so he reached the halfway point on a Monday.

8. 1500 g
To work out how much 1 part is, divide the amount of beef by 4.
2 kg = 2000 g, and $2000 \div 4 = 500$ g.
If 1 part is 500 g, and she needs 3 parts pork, she'll need 500 g $\times 3 = 1500$ g of pork.

9. 7
Subtract the mass of the lorry from the mass that the bridge can support to work out how much the lorry can carry over the bridge: $21\ 000 - 6000 = 15\ 000$ kg. Now divide this by the mass of one crate to find the number of crates that can be carried:
$15\ 000 \div 2000 = 7.5$, so 7 full crates can be carried across.

10. B
Substitute $r = 70$ into the formula:
$8 \times 70 + 50 = 560 + 50 = 610$.

Puzzles 9 — page 79

Floorplan Problem
There are many ways you could have arranged the rooms. Your floorplan might look a bit different to the example below, but the rooms should have the following areas:
Living room — 48 squares
Dining room — 36 squares
Kitchen and garage — 24 squares each
Bathroom —12 squares

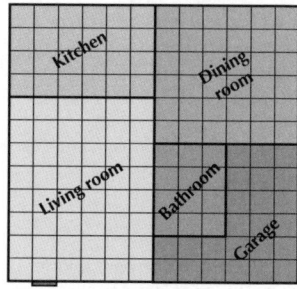

One to Seven
There are several ways that the numbers could have been arranged. For example:

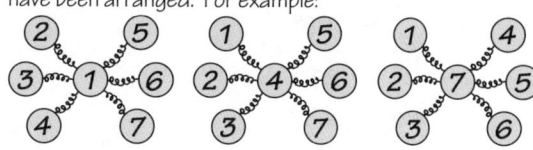

Test 24 — page 80-82

1. B
The 4 in 14 792 stands for 4 thousands. When rounding, always look at the digit to the right of the number you're rounding. Because the 7 to the right of the 4 thousands is higher than 5, round up the number to 15 000.

2. £100
The total prize after 3 weeks is £175. To find the original prize amount, subtract £25 for every week:
£175 – £25 × 3 = £100.

3. C
A quick way to do this question is to spot the three numbers whose units add up to a multiple of 10. The only option that does this is 9, 17 and 34: 9 + 7 + 4 = 20. So you just have to check that it is right: 9 + 17 + 34 = 60.

4. 210 minutes
The train travels 100 km every hour, so in 3 hours it will travel 3 × 100 = 300 km. Then it will take half an hour to travel an extra 50 km, giving a total time of 3 hours 30 minutes. In minutes, this is: 3 × 60 + 30 = 180 + 30 = 210 minutes.

5. 3
For the children she needs 10 × 250 ml = 2500 ml. For the adults she needs 4 × 400 ml = 1600 ml. So in total she needs 2500 + 1600 = 4100 ml. Each bottle is 2 litres = 2000 ml. 2 bottles will contain a total of 4000 ml, which isn't enough, and 3 bottles will contain 6000 ml, which is enough. So she needs 3 bottles.

6. 1 hour 15 minutes
The news is on for 45 minutes (6:00 pm - 6:45 pm). The weather is on for 15 minutes (6:45 pm - 7:00 pm), so together they come to 1 hour. The acrobatics is also on for 15 minutes (7:00 pm - 7:15 pm), so José watches TV for 1 hour 15 minutes.

7. C
To find out how much of the $^2/_5$ she put in each box, divide $^2/_5$ by 4. To divide a fraction by a whole number, you multiply the denominator by the whole number and keep the numerator as it is: $^2/_5 \div 4 = ^2/_{20}$ (as 5 × 4 = 20). $^2/_{20}$ can be simplified to $^1/_{10}$.

8. D
Jonah travelled 6 km between 11:00 and 12:00 (12 – 6 = 6). He stayed in the same place between 12:00 and 13:00, but then travelled 4 km between 13:00 and 13:30 (12 – 8 = 4). 6 + 4 = 10 km.

9. A
£1.10 = 110p. So for x hours Sharon pays 110 × x = 110x pence.

10. 24°
The shapes are regular, so all the angles inside the pentagons are equal, and all the angles inside the hexagon are equal.

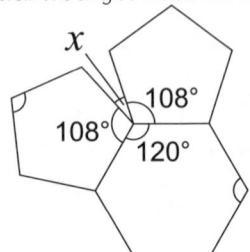

The angles round a point add up to 360°, so x + 108° + 120° + 108° = 360°.
x + 336° = 360°.
x = 360° – 336° = 24°

Test 25 — page 83-85

1. A
To find the fraction of grey cats, subtract $^1/_2$ and $^1/_4$ from 1: 1 – $^1/_2$ – $^1/_4$ = $^1/_4$.

2. D
Shape 4 is a triangle (3 sides), so this rules out C. Shapes 2 and 5 only have right angles, so this rules out A, B and E. Shapes 1 and 3 have two obtuse angles and two acute angles. So D is correct.

3. B
Kate saves £1.50 per week, so she saves £1.50 × 2 = £3 every two weeks. Work out how many lots of £3 she has saved so far: £30 ÷ £3 = 10 lots. So she has saved for 10 lots of two weeks, which gives a total of 10 × 2 = 20 weeks.

4. 29
Add up the number of children that own 6 or more pens: 6 children own 6 pens, 7 own 7 pens, 9 own 8 pens, 5 own 9 pens and 2 own 10 pens. 6 + 7 + 9 + 5 + 2 = 29.

5. E
He parks 2 hours per day, so will spend 2 × 50p = £1 per day. Over a year, this will be £275 (as he parks for 275 days), so the saving will be £275 – £250 = £25.

6. 10 °C
Add up all the temperatures then divide them by the number of readings. 8 + 9 + 11 + 13 + 9 = 50. There are five readings, so the mean is 50 ÷ 5 = 10 °C.

7. 200
The circumference of the wheel is 150 cm, which is the same as 1.5 m. This means that the wheel makes one complete turn every 1.5 m. To work out how many it makes in 300 m, divide 300 by 1.5: 300 ÷ 1.5 = 200 complete turns.

8. 40 cm
Write down the multiples of 5 to show the height of the 5 cm-block tower each time a new block is added:
5, 10, 15, 20, 25, 30, 35, 40, 45, ...
Also write down the multiples of 8 to show the height of the 8 cm-block tower each time a new block is added:
8, 16, 24, 32, 40, 48, ...
40 appears in both lists, so the towers will each be 40 cm high when they are the same height for the first time.

9. C
The proportion of fruit juice in the can be rewritten as $^{49.5}/_{330}$. So the amount of juice is higher than 10% ($^{33}/_{330}$), but lower than 20% ($^{66}/_{330}$). This means it must contain between 10% and 20%, so it must be C. You can check the percentage by adding 10% + 5% of 330: 33 + 16.5 = 49.5. So the answer is 15%.

10.
Put the numbers into the equation that you're given.
Volume = $^1/_3$ × area of the base × height,
so 4 = $^1/_3$ × area of the base × 3.
$^1/_3$ × 3 = 1, so 4 = area of the base. The base is square, so the side length must be 2 cm (as 2 × 2 = 4).

Puzzles 10 — page 86

Trapped By a Trickster

The answers to the clues are:

 = 15   = 8   = 30   ▨ = 24

In order to escape, you need to step on these 4 stones:

15 + 30	30 − 8	24 − 15	24 + 8
45	**22**	**9**	**32**
8 − 24	15 + 24	30 + 8	8 − 15
−16	**39**	**38**	**−7**
15 + 8	15 − 30	15 − 24	24 + 30
23	**−15**	**−9**	**54**

Test 26 — pages 87-89

1. C
Raymond's time must be somewhere between 19.025 and 19.134. 19.205 is too big, because its tenths value is 2. 19.000 and 19.010 are too small, because their tenths values are 0 and their hundredths values are less than 2. 19.150 is too big, because its tenths value is 1 and its hundredths value is greater than 3. So 19.123 is the only value which fits.

2. B
```
  3 6 . 9 9
  1 0 . 2 9
+  3 . 5 0
─────────
  5 0 . 7 8
    1 1  1
```

3. 0.8 m
Read across from the height of the bars to the y-axis to find the length of each neck. Goliath's neck is 2 m long. Yeti's neck is 1.2 m long. 2 − 1.2 = 0.8, so Goliath's neck is 0.8 m longer.

4. 160
The number of bacteria increases every 20 minutes from 10 to 20, 40, 80 etc. The rule is to double the previous term, so the bacteria are doubling every 20 minutes. After another 20 minutes, the bacteria will have doubled from 80 to 80 × 2 = 160.

5. 4200 litres
21 ÷ 3 = 7, so there will be 7 times as much water flowing over the waterfall in 21 seconds than in 3 seconds: 600 litres × 7 = 4200 litres.

6. 30%
First find the total weight of all the ingredients:
280 + 60 + 40 + 20 = 400 g.
Now find the total weight of sugar:
60 + 40 + 20 = 120 g.
So 120 g out of 400 g is sugar. As a fraction, this is $^{120}/_{400}$. Dividing the numerator and denominator by 4 gives $^{30}/_{100}$, which is equivalent to 30%.

7. $^1/_{40}$
There are 30 days in June. Eliza eats $^3/_4$ of the jar in June, so she eats $^3/_4 ÷ 30 = ^3/_{120}$ of the jar on average each day (4 × 30 = 120). Both 3 and 120 are divisible by 3, so you can simplify the fraction to $^1/_{40}$.

8. B
Kara gets off at 6:30 pm,
Ryan gets off 15 minutes earlier (6:15 pm)
and Sharon gets off 10 minutes after Ryan (6:25 pm).
A is false, as Sharon gets off at 6:25 pm.
B is correct.
C is false, as Sharon gets off the train before Kara.
D is false, as Sharon spends 30 minutes on the train.
E is false, as Kara gets off the train 5 minutes after Sharon.

9. C
5 miles = 8 km, so to convert a distance from miles to km, divide by 5 then multiply by 8.
40 ÷ 5 = 8. 8 × 8 = 64 km.
So to work out how far she has travelled so far, subtract this distance from the total distance. Using partitioning:
6076 − 64 = 6076 − 60 − 4 = 6016 − 4 = 6012 km.

10. D
You can fit four triangles in each row, with some spare room. There is space left over, but not for a whole tile. You can fit four of these rows in the square (as 4 × 25 mm = 100 mm).

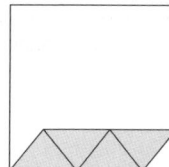 

So you can fit 4 × 4 = 16 whole triangles on the square board.

Test 27 — pages 90-92

1. £17.00 or £17
The 0 in £17.03 is being rounded. 3 is smaller than 5, so £17.03 rounds down to £17.00.

2. 5
In 3 boxes, there are 15 × 3 = 45 chocolates in total.
The chocolates are shared between 9 people (Dwayne + each of his 8 friends), so each person gets 45 ÷ 9 = 5 chocolates.

3. E
There are 12 edges on a cube. If each edge is 2 m long, then Simon needs 2 × 12 = 24 m of lights.

4. D
Using the column method for multiplication:
```
    2 . 4 5
  ×       5
  ─────────
  1 2 . 2 5
      2 2
```

5. £3.15
Find the total value for each coin:
50 × 2 = 100, 20 × 4 = 80, 10 × 8 = 80, 5 × 4 = 20,
2 × 10 = 20, 1 × 15 = 15.
Add the total values for each coin together:
100 + 80 + 80 + 20 + 20 + 15 = 315p = £3.15.

6. 7.5
The bar for Monday is 8 squares high, so each square must represent 1 penguin. Add up the totals for each day from the chart to find the total number of penguins:
8 + 7 + 9 + 6 = 30 penguins. Now divide by 4 to find the mean:
30 ÷ 4 = 7.5.

7. 6
Half of 32 is 32 ÷ 2 = 16, so 16 people chose envelope C.
4 more people chose B than A, so if x is the number of people who chose A, the number of people who chose B is $(x + 4)$.
16 people chose either A or B, so $2x + 4 = 16$.
Subtracting 4 from each side, $2x = 12$.
Dividing both sides by 2, $x = 6$, so 6 people chose A.

8. 10:25 am
12 hours after 7:55 pm on Saturday is 7:55 am on Sunday.
You only need to add on another 2 hours 30 minutes to make the 14 hours 30 minutes in total. 2 hours 30 minutes after 7:55 am is 10:25 am on Sunday.

9. B
Cleaning fluid and water are combined in a ratio of 1:4, so 1 part out of every 5 parts of the mixture is cleaning fluid.
Fiona needs 1.5 l of the mixture. 1.5 l = 1500 ml, so she will need 1500 ÷ 5 = 300 ml of cleaning fluid.

10. C
29 is a prime number, so 29 cards cannot be dealt evenly between a group of players, unless there are 29 players or 1 player in the game. Each player needs at least 2 cards, so there can't be 29 players. There is a group of friends playing the game, so there can't be just 1 player. So there cannot be 29 cards in the pack.

Test 28 — pages 93-95

1. 480 g
It's rounded to the nearest ten, so look in the ones column.
It's a 5, so round up to 480 g.

2. $1/4$
18 out of 72 as a fraction is $18/72$. This can be simplified by dividing the numerator and denominator by 18 = $1/4$.

3. 250
Calculate how many books there will be by adding up all the pictures apart from the non-fiction books: there are 11 whole pictures and 3 half pictures. 11 + 1.5 = 12.5.
Each picture represents 20 books, so there will be 12.5 × 20 = 250 books.

4. D
The star's perimeter is made from two sides of each of the octagons. Two sides have a perimeter of 2 × 5 = 10 cm. There are eight octagons, so the total perimeter is: 8 × 10 = 80 cm.

5. 60
You need to find out how many large boxes you could get for £14, as the price per piece of fudge is much lower than the small box. The most large boxes you could get is 2:
£14 ÷ £5 = 2 with a remainder of £4.
The most small boxes you could get with £4 = 4 ÷ 2 = 2.
So 2 of each box. Then add up the total number of pieces of fudge: there are 24 pieces in each large box and 6 in each small box, so (24 × 2) + (6 × 2) = 48 + 12 = 60 pieces.

6. D
The most accurate way to read off a line graph is to use a point where the graph intersects the grid.
E.g. for 12 apples, Antoine needs = 300 g of sugar.
So for 4 apples, he needs 300 ÷ 3 = 100 g of sugar (as 12 ÷ 3 =4). This means he needs 100 × 2 = 200 g of sugar for 8 apples, so D is correct.

7. B
If Jake is x years old, Jayden is $(x + 13)$ years old.
The total of their two ages is 45, so $2x + 13 = 45$.
Subtracting 13 from each side, $2x = 32$.
Dividing both sides by 2, $x = 16$. So Jake is 16 years old.

8. C
Along each side there are nine triangles. There are three sides, so 3 × 9 = 27. But at each corner, two triangles have been counted twice. So 2 × 3 = 6 triangles have been counted twice.
So there are 27 − 6 = 21 triangles in total. You can check this by completing the drawing and then counting the triangles:

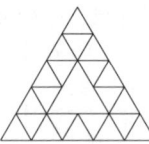

9. D
To find the number of people whose favourite festive food was Brussels sprouts, turn the ratio into a fraction: $4/15$.
Divide 285 by the denominator: 285 ÷ 15 = 19. Then multiply by the numerator: 19 × 4 = 76. 76 people said Brussels sprouts were their favourite festive food.

10. 16:15
First work out 1 hour 20 minutes before 17:10 — this will give you the actual time that the watch stopped.
1 hour before 17:10 is 16:10. And 20 minutes before this is 15:50. So the watch stopped at 15:50. But the watch is 25 minutes fast — it always shows the time 25 minutes ahead. Adding 25 minutes onto 15:50 gives a time of 16:15.

Puzzles 11 — page 96

Conversion Confusion

Names	Time spent	Time spent (hours and minutes)
Rania & Mark	237 minutes	3 hours 57 minutes
Tom & Bea	From 10:30 am to 4:00 pm (with a 30 minute lunch)	5 hours
Mollie & Sajid	$2/3$ of 9 hours	6 hours
Kurt & Shirley	Three 90-minute sessions	4 hours 30 minutes

Mollie and Sajid practised for the longest time.

Find the Prize
The star prize is in the box labelled 108.

Test 29 — pages 97-99

1. 13 000
The number of packets he's ordered is 13 × 10 = 130
The number of paperclips included is:
130 × 100 = 13 000.

2. 60%
Multiply the numerator and denominator by 20 (to make the denominator 100). 3 × 20 = 60, 5 × 20 = 100, so $3/5 = 60/100$. As a percentage is out of 100, $3/5 = 60\%$.

3. A
Because the multiple choice answers are very different from one another, the quickest way to answer this question is to use rounding.
1.7 m rounds to 2 m to the nearest metre,
£7.10 rounds to £7 to the nearest pound.
2 × 7 = 14. The only answer around 14 is £12.07.

4. B
The scales will balance if the weight of the potatoes equals the weight of the compost. The six bags of potatoes will weigh 1.5 × 6 = 9 kg. Each sack of compost weights 4.5 kg, so you need 9 ÷ 4.5 = 2 sacks.

5. 3 litres
The amount of water in ml that Gordon uses is double the amount of rice in grams. 1.5 kg = 1500 g, so he uses 2 × 1500 = 3000 ml of water, which is equal to 3 litres.

6. 10
When there are 4 cards, the mean is 5. This means that the total of the numbers on the 4 cards = 4 × 5 = 20.
After Letisha adds another card, the mean becomes 6, so the total of the numbers on the 5 cards = 6 × 5 = 30.
The difference between the two totals is the number that will be on the last card to be added: 30 – 20 = 10, so a 10 must have been added.

7. A
There is 60 g of protein in 100 g of biltong, so you will need 300 ÷ 60 = 5 times as much biltong to get 300 g of protein.
So you need 5 × 100 g = 500 g of biltong.
There is 250 g of biltong in a packet, so you need 500 ÷ 250 = 2 packets of biltong.

8. C
There will be 9 rows, each with 9 trees, giving a total of 9 × 9 = 81 trees planted. It could help to draw the trees in a grid, as shown below.

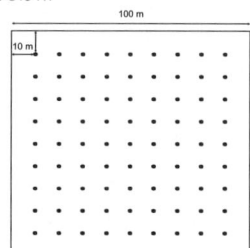

9. C
In one hour, the hour hand moves one number around the clock face. There are 12 numbers on a clock, so in one hour the hour hand moves 360 ÷ 12 = 30°. So in a quarter of an hour, the hour hand moves a quarter of this amount: 30° ÷ 4 = 7.5°.

10. 12 cm
If the height of the toy block is 1 cm, the width is 2 cm and the length is 4 cm, then you can fit 20 ÷ 4 = 5 blocks along the length of the toy box. You can fit 8 ÷ 2 = 4 blocks along the width of the toy box, so on one layer of the toy box you can fit 5 × 4 = 20 toy blocks.
If you can fit 240 blocks in the box then you need 240 ÷ 20 = 12 layers of blocks. Each block is 1 cm high, so 12 layers are 12 × 1 cm = 12 cm high. So the toy box is 12 cm high. (You could stack the blocks in a different positions, i.e. all on their side or on their end, and you would still get the same answer.)

Test 30 — pages 100-102

1. –2.5 °C
2 °C – 4.5 °C = –2.5 °C.

2. D
100 people each won £346.47, so the total amount won is £346.47 × 100 = £34 647.

3. A
Work out how many blueberries she has eaten after each hour. Every hour, she eats 2 more blueberries than the previous hour.

09:00   10:00   11:00   12:00   13:00   14:00

So at 14:00, she's eaten all 42 blueberries.

4. A
An equilateral triangle has three equal interior angles. A parallelogram, an isosceles triangle and a rhombus all have 2 different sizes of interior angle. A kite has 3 different sizes of interior angle, e.g. in the kite below, A and C are the same, but B and D are both different.

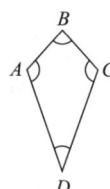

5. 25 minutes
Each division on the y-axis is worth 1 km, so each quarter division is worth 0.25 km. Read across from 1.75 km on the y-axis until you reach the line, then read down until you reach the x-axis:

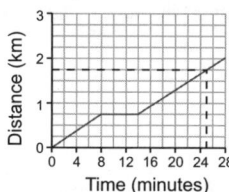

The dashed line falls $1/4$ of the way between 24 and 28, so it takes the hiker 25 minutes to reach the field.

6. 35
There are 14 hazelnut chocolates, arranged into groups of 2. 14 ÷ 2 = 7, so there must be 7 groups of chocolates altogether. Each group contains 5 orange chocolates, so there is a total of 7 × 5 = 35 orange chocolates.

7. D
If the pentagon has a perimeter of 550 m, then one side has length 550 ÷ 5 = 110 m. Each fence panel is 10 m wide, so you need 110 ÷ 10 = 11 panels to fence one side.

8. £113.42

```
  2 4 . 5 9
×         3
-----------
  7 3 . 7 7
  1 1 2
```

£73.77 + £39.65 = £113.42

9. 10 km
First, find out how many lots of 150 g there are in 15 kg.
15 kg = 15 000 g, so there are 15 000 ÷ 150 = 100 lots.
So he can walk 100 lots of 100 m before the sandbag is empty.
100 × 100 m = 10 000 m, which is 10 km.

10. D
Find what angle the sector would be for 1 person by finding $1/40$ of 360°. You know from your times tables that 36 ÷ 4 = 9, so 360° ÷ 40 = 9°. So for 22 people, the sector will have an angle of 9 × 22 = 198°.

Test 31 — pages 103-105

1. B
The order should be: 10.67, 10.73, 11.03, 11.1, 11.11.
So the one out of order is 11.1.

2. 6 kg
40 ÷ 10 = 4, so he needs to buy four times as much flour for 40 students than he does for 10 students.
So Mr Baker has to buy 1500 g × 4 = 6000 g.
1000 g = 1 kg, so he needs 6000 ÷ 1000 = 6 kg.

3. 21
To find $^7/_8$ of 24, first find $^1/_8$ of 24. 24 ÷ 8 = 3.
If $^1/_8$ of 24 is 3, then $^7/_8$ = 3 × 7 = 21.

4. 1 : 3
7 of the 28 pupils wear glasses, meaning 21 don't wear glasses. As a ratio, this is 7 : 21. This can be simplified to 1 : 3 by dividing the 7 and 21 by 7 = 1 : 3.

5. 1.95 cm
Using the column method of addition, add the straw lengths:

```
   1 3 . 4
       4 . 4
 + 1 0 . 2 5
 ───────────
   2 8 . 0 5
   1
```

So the total length of the straws is 28.05 cm.
Subtract this from 30 cm to find the distance:
Using partitioning, 28.05 breaks into 28 + 0.05.
30 − 28 = 2, 2 − 0.05 = 1.95 cm.

6. B
Find $^3/_4$ of 300 ml. 300 ÷ 4 × 3 = 75 × 3 = 225 ml.
So the dispenser will be refilled when 225 ml has been used.
5 ml is dispensed on each use, so 225 ml will have been used after 225 ÷ 5 = 45 uses.

7. B
The area of the piece of wood is 4 × 4 = 16 m². Find the total area of the four corner desks by subtracting the area of the circular table: 16 − 7 = 9 m². To find the area of one corner desk, divide by four: 9 ÷ 4 = 2.25 m².

8. D
The graph is misleading because the scale on the y-axis is uneven, making the increase in price look much worse than it is.

9. 121
Sachin needs to divide the blocks equally between 13 people (himself and 12 friends), so you need to work out 1573 ÷ 13. The sum involves dividing by a 2-digit number, so it's easiest to do long division.

```
          1 2 1
   1 3 ) 1 5 7 3
         -1 3 ↓
          ───
            2 7
          - 2 6 ↓
            ───
              1 3
            - 1 3
              ───
                0
```

So Sachin needs to give 121 blocks to each friend.

10. C
Each sheet of paper makes 4 pages in the booklet.
So for x pages, Gregory needs $^x/_4$ sheets of paper.
The advert is an extra 1 sheet of paper, so in total Gregory needs $^x/_4$ + 1 sheets of paper.

Puzzles 12 — page 106

Ghostly Goings-on...
Your timeline should look like this:

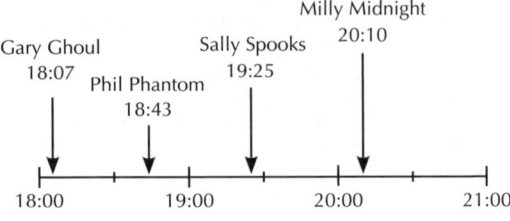